Unknow

Also by D.M.Thomas:

See also www.dmthomasonline.com
        www.don-whitehotel.blogspot.com

Unknown Shores

Collected SF Poems

D.M. Thomas

Published by bluechrome publishing 2009

2 4 6 8 10 9 7 5 3 1

Copyright © D.M. Thomas 2009

First published in Great Britain in 2009 by
bluechrome publishing
PO Box 109,
Portishead, Bristol. BS20 7ZJ

www.bluechrome.co.uk

A CIP catalogue record for this book is available from the
British Library

ISBN 978-1-906061-54-8

Acknowledgements

Unknown Shores, Missionary, A Conversation upon the Shadow, Fire-victims, Tithonus, Symbiosis, Two Sonnets from Drifting Worlds, Mercury, S.F., A Dead Planet, Cygnus A, Hera's Spring, The Strait, and Elegy for an Android were first published in *Modern Poets 11* (Pengun, 1968);   Two Voices, Ge, and The Head-Rape, in *Two Voices* (Cape Goliard, 1968);   Computer 70, in *Logan Stone* (Cape Goliard, 1971);   Blue Shift, in *Love and Other Deaths* (Paul Elek, 1975);   Christ on Palomar, in *The Puberty Tree* (Penguin, 1992).

Some of the poems evolved from stories by such SF prose masters as Ray Bradbury, Arthur C.Clarke, Tom Godwin, Damon Knight and James J.Schmidt.

Previously uncollected, Seeking a Suitable Donor first appeared in *The New S.F.,* ed. Langdon Jones (Hutchinson, 1969); and Mr Black's Poems of Innocence, in *Best SF Stories from New Worlds 6*, ed. Michael Moorcock (Panther, 1970).

Contents

Introduction

The poems in this collection, mostly written between 1965 and 1970, form a distinct phase in my creative life. I was at the time an avid reader of science fiction; there seemed to me an opportunity for a poet to explore that territory also. I suppose, in retrospect, I was dimly conscious that I was not a lyrical poet but needed a strong narrative element: an interesting conflict within myself which, many years later, led to my writing novels: yet novels, I have always felt, which have their wellspring in poetry, myth and symbol.

The science fiction stories I read struck me as an exploration of myths –myths of the future. They engaged with the sudden, sometimes exhilarating, sometimes frightening, opening up of possibilities in human life. I don't imagine Jane Austen or Dickens thought human life would change essentially during or after their lifetimes; but in the second half of the twentieth century all things seemed possible. The scientists and technocrats were Prometheus, stealing fire from the gods, taking control of their –and our—destiny.

The DNA code had been cracked, giving us the potential to interfere with our genes, perhaps mix them with those of other creatures, as is now happening. The discovery of planets circling other stars made us aware of the strong probability that there could be life on some of them; observatories were given over to the express purpose of looking for intelligent signals from outer space. For a while we seemed to expect such signals any year or any day. Hearts were being transplanted. Even the idea that people might live forever no longer belonged simply to Greek myth –as in the story of Tithonus, wonderfully explored in Tennyson's poem of that name—but could conceivably happen. Man landed on the moon. It was a mind-blowing time.

The visual media were becoming more and more powerful, often changing the reality which the camera was supposed to be recording faithfully. So, an execution in Vietnam might be delayed for a few moments while a cameraman put in a fresh film. We were beginning to become a watched generation –and today there are more CCTV cameras in Britain than there are people.

Even Eros was changing, becoming more scientifically and technologically determined, with the contraceptive pill and vibrating 'sex toys'. It was ironic that the first moon-walks were called EVA – extra-vehicular activity. Eve, the mother goddess, had been distorted and masculinized. Despite the coming of flower power, Dr Strangelove still held the real power. The feminine, the *yin*, had never seemed more repressed.

There was, in that decade of the Cuban Missile Crisis-- a distinct chance that man would destroy all life on the planet. One lived with a constant, if mostly unconscious, fear. Reading my poems of that period again, I am struck by how many were symbols of my own fear.

My *Tithonus* is simply a brain being kept artificially alive, separate from the body. In *Hera's Spring,* immortality is achieved by an endless cycle of existence on different stars, but at the cost of multiple bereavements. In *A Conversation upon the Shadow*, two lovers on a planet with six suns cherish the fact that they don't know *everything* about each other, allowing them to retain their individual identity. The question of the identity and integrity of the individual is also central to *The Strait.* This long poem explores the great love-story of Tristan and Yseult in a futuristic way. Thanks to the invention of plastic humanoids which can duplicate anyone, Tristan is able to take a copy of his mistress with him to the moon, to solace him, while the real Yseult stays behind with her jealous husband. But after a while, which *is* the real Yseult? The humanoid model certainly believes she is.

The epigraph for *The Strait* is from a short story by Ray Bradbury. It sets a date for these plastic creatures: 1990, which was a trifle over-optimistic, or pessimistic! But artificial life is certainly on the way. .

Quite suddenly in the early 1970's, I felt a revulsion towards reading science fiction. I don't know why; it was like the onset of an allergy, comparable to my sudden aversion around that time to my favourite menthol cigarettes.

In terms of my poetry, I found I increasingly wanted to explore other, more realistic, themes. It was a healthy urge. The movement out of writing SF poems was a gradual process. A key moment of change is represented by the long narrative poem *Two Voices*. In it, I interwove a 'traditional' SF story with the wanderings of a pregnant girl near the Los Alamos nuclear test centre in New Mexico. The astronauts, in space, watch with horror as their mother earth explodes. The girl agonisingly contemplates the choice of abortion or adoption, and is also tormented by why her father took his life. In so doing he has – equally with her unscupulous lover-- killed her emotionally; while the sterile desert and Los Alamos make her fearful of ultimate destruction, a 'third crowing of the male cock' in her life. The astronauts meanwhile –if 'meanwhile' means anything in space-time—create the illusion of their long-dead wives pharmaceutically. .

Mr Black's Poems of Innocence was inspired by a radio documentary in 1968 about a mute schizophrenic, a Mr Blake, being treated with operant conditioning. The treatment was well-intentioned, but struck me as appallingly cold and uncaring. I felt the patient's namesake, the poet William, would have also hated the 'single vision and Newton's sleep' of the operant conditioner. It encouraged me to have my fictional patient, Mr Black, express internally his pain and longing in Blakean imagery. The resulting work was first published in an SF anthology, but has never previously appeared in any of my collections.

Only a few sections of *Computer 70: Dreams & Lovepoems* continue in the traditional SF *genre*, often as symbols of aspects of love; but the mindset of this work, of man seeming to be programming his own destruction, and of 'the male cock crowing', is still the same as in my 'pure' SF. In this transitional work I was attempting to fuse the (feared) future with the past and present, the historical with the personal: John Keats's voyage to Italy in 1820; the death by drowning of Mary Jo Kopechne in 1969, in a car being driven by Senator Edward Kennedy; a Vietnam vet's guilty memories; the first moon landings; Godard's coldly brilliant film 'Alphaville'; the shadow of nuclear holocaust. At its conclusion, the werewolf legend, JFK's assassination, and the Boston Strangler –active in 1963—make an appearance.

I have removed from *Computer 70* a few individual poems which now strike me as not truly belonging to it. Apart from this, all the work in this collection is as it first appeared.

Re-reading the poems, in most cases for the first time in thirty years, has been a strange experience. It's as though I'm meeting an unknown poet. I hardly recognise the self I was then. Yet it *was* me; and I am grateful to bluechrome for this opportunity to bring all the poems together in one book.

                 D.M.Thomas
                 Truro, Cornwall, UK
                 2009

Unknown Shores

AFTER THÉOPHILE GAUTIER

Okay, my starsick beauty! –
blue jeans and tilting breasts,
child of Canaverel –
where would you like to go?

Shall we set course for Mars,
or Venus's green sea,
Aldebaran the golden,
or Tycho Brahe's Nova,
or the moons of Sagitta,
or Vega's colonies?

School-minching, bronze Diane,
bane of the launching-pads –
I may not ask again:
wherever you would go

my rocket-head can turn
at will to your command –
to pluck the flowers of snow
that grow on Pluto, or
Capella-wards, to pluck
the roots of asphodel?

I may not ask again:
where would you like to go?

Have you a star, she says,
O any faithful sun
where love does not eclipse?
… (The countdown slurs and slips).
- Ah child, if that star shines,
it is in chartless skies,

I do not know of such!
But come, where will you go?

13

Missionary

A harsh entry I had of it, Grasud;
the tiny shuttle strained to its limits
by radiation-belts, dust storms,
not to mention the pitiless heat which
hit it on plunging into the atmosphere
- its fire-shield clean vaporized; and then,
on landing, the utter cold and stillness
of a mountain-slope, cedar-trees and
what they call
snow. As I went numbly through the
routine I could do in my sleep –
mentalizing myself, smothering
my body and the shuttle in a
defensive neutrino-screen, hiding them
securely in the snow,
I looked up and, between the branches
of the cedars, could see
the mother-ship sliding away through
the dark, like an unfixed star, westwards
to its other destinations: that was
the worst moment of all, Grasud! I'd have
called it back! So lonely, such an alien
world they'd left me in. Goodbye, Lagash!
goodbye, Theremon! fare well! (But no
voice now even to make a gesture against
the silence.)
              Then the agonizingly slow
descent, towards the village,
my spirit dark, already missing
not only Theremon and Lagash, but
that other friend, my body's familiar
chemistry. By now I felt my
vaunted courage ebbing, Grasud; I think
those years of training
alone forced me to go on, into the village,
into the houses, inns, into

- after much vain searching – a ripened
womb; there superseding
(not without a pang) its foetus-spirit.
How black that airlock,
after the six suns of our own system,
I needn't tell you. Even space,
in recollection, seemed a blaze of
supernovas. But I settled to my task,
wrestling to get on terms with carbon
compounds fearsomely different from
the synthetic ones I'd practised in.
Of course, as I was born and the years
passed, it seemed as natural to go
on man's two legs as on our Vardian
limbs. But when these pains eased,
one far bitterer grew: my seeds were cast
on stony ground; the more
I exhorted,
- the more I spoke, obliquely, of
the many mansions of our Vardian
Commonwealth, and of the place
that could be theirs – the more it
seemed those simple, instinctive creatures
lied, stole, slandered, fornicated,
killed…. Grasud, how often, sick with
failure, only the words of Vrak
sustained me – 'a world lies in your hands.'
That was the time he
sent for the three of us when
all ears were ringing with the news of
the three life-planets found in
NDT 1065. If we had hopes,
we masked them. His words to us, for
all that's happened, I'll hoard always.
Thoorin, Lagash, Theremon,' I hear him
saying, 'I'm sending *you*…. You're young,
but this is what you've trained for, bio-
enlightenment. You've done well.'
And then – 'a world lies in your hands.'

So, Grasud, I toiled. In the end
I tried too hard; the time of space-
rendezvous was almost come. Anyway,
they killed me. I loved them, and they
killed me.
                    Yes, it was hard,
as you can well imagine,
on the return-journey, to avoid feeling
the faintest warp of
jealousy, as Theremon and
Lagash talked with
the happy emissaries of their
planets. – What does Vrak say?   He is
kind, promises – after this loathsome
rest – another
chance, though not of course on that
planet. My 'inability' (he avoids
the word failure) to raise them
ethically to the point where we could
safely announce ourselves, proves, he
says, there's no point trying again
for a few thousand years. Meanwhile,
he suggests, maybe some of my words
will start to bear fruit…. He is kind!
His last words were 'Forget about it,
Thoorin; enjoy your stay on
Atar.' Forget!
with the relaxed faces of my friends a
perpetual thorn!

A Conversation upon the Shadow

When strangers see through you,
it is a lover's right to be blinded.
URAAN PROVERB

                ... Epsilon
sets; and minutes later
Delta sinks in the east,
blazing orange sphere.
Now, if ever on Uraa,
stars might shine down, as
Gamma alone remains
poised in the sky: small,
cool, slate-blue. But still
it is too bright for
stars. Through the parched
meadows, tinting blue,
Ilkaar and Shaara walk;
moving their lips in speech
since their wiry coronets
impede the flow of thoughts.

'Shaara, now that all our suns
but one have set, shadows
flow from us. Do they not
shape for you the mental
shadows, psi-screens, which
as lovers we are
privileged to cast
upon each other? Just
as for these three hours
we walked with no shadow
here, so, in the years
of our cool friendship we
revealed all thoughts to the
other; but now, 'tis not so.
This gloom-hour is loveliest.'

17

Shaara sighs, nodding accord.
'Yes, yes, to be so
intimate in the body,
and as intimate in the
mind as one is with strangers,
would be … unbearable.
I suppose there must have
been shadows like these all day
in our Primal Garden
when only Alpha had been
created, and half the time
there was a thing called night - '

' – By Primal Garden you mean,
I take it, the remote world
our ancestors flew from! …'

She lifts her eyebrows in
smiling exasperation –
'Oh well, we won't go into
science versus religion
just now! - ' (digging her nails
into his palm) – 'anyway,
I'd have been happier then,
I think, - with night, whatever
that was, and the people were
un-telepathic, *walking
in darkness*. Well, at least
I'm allowed to keep
my thoughts from *you*, allowed
not to know yours…. *Kala*!'
(murmuring the word of
thanksgiving, touching the
sun-discs round her ebony
throat).

'But for how long, Shaara?
For how long can we resist
the temptation to strip off
the psi-screens and show all,
not in indifference this time,
but in a lust for candour?'

'Never, Ilkaar!'

                        ... Beta
rises; and an hour later,
Alpha heaves in the west,
brilliant white giant.
Epsilon... Delta.
The shadows are purged
from the black, naked bodies
of the walking lovers.
Now, if ever on Uraa,
there is absolute candour.

Fire-victims

When her wheeled-chair parted the
electron-portals, and under
the indulgent gaze of the
medical-staff they flew, too
long in purdah of their casts,
into each other's arms, then
laughingly, wonderingly
touched each tenderly grafted
cadaver-tissue – lips, eyes, and
facial skin for Kadmos; hands,
and dorsal skin, and breasts, Har-
monia – both caught, but lightly
put out of their minds, a hiss
new to their mythically
straitlaced union: Jealousy?

Tithonus

And finally, ladies and gentlemen, perhaps in his quiet way
As exciting as many of our other exhibits,
Just group around and let me introduce you to
Our very first immortal *homo sapiens*.
Yes, here we have – but a word of caution, sir,
These tubes are delicate – the first *immortal*.
Let that word chime. Forget Jesus, forget
 - Well, all the other man-gods of pre-history,
And fix your eyes instead on Edgar L. Cummings
As he floats here, bottled greyly in solution.
Death, Thou art Dead!
And isn't that typical scientific hooh-hah for something
So unimpressive – a mere pulsing sponge!
I don't blame you – But believe me when I say
That all Man's dreams of immortality,
 - Penny for old Charon, them pearly gates,
Or some lotus-isle where falls not rain or hail –
Are here made coldly but thrillingly *fact*.
He just can't die! ...- oh, barring some cosmic disaster.
Our Institute, you've seen, 's impregnable –
Fire-proof, bomb-proof, radiation-proof,
Sterilized; and when in a few billion billion years
Our sun threatens to blow up, he'll be whipped off
Like all the rest, to some more genial star.

Professor Wiggins will perhaps fill you in on
His case-history later – you can see
She's rather busy fussing over his welfare as usual!
Miss Wiggins, my colleague in the Department of Tithonics,
Was actually present twenty years ago,
In student capacity, when Professor Joseph performed
The historic excision. Briefly though: Edgar L. Cummings,
Born 1961, transfigured, so to speak, 2025
While dying, in coma, of arterio-sclerosis;
No relative surviving to worry about names,

21

Re-christened Tithonus, after an old greek story
Which you will find briefly summarized on this plaque.
Unfortunately we can't provide an Eos,
Unless indeed Miss Wiggins – good EVENING, professor! –
Could be said to fill that category…. She certainly clucks
Tenderly over him all hours of the day and night,
Spends less and less time at her East Side apartment,
Burns midnight fluorescence rivalling the splendour
Of her own auburn – *Why Dawn, I believe you're*
        BLUSHING!
Well, well - ! many a true word in jest, folks!
You'll bear me out, we've *proved* a real Heart beats
Under that tall and intellectual white,
That those spiky heels take the strain of feminine
        Passions!…
What's that? You'll get me later?… I'll look forward…!
Seriously, ladies and gentlemen, I know the question
You all must be dying to pose: in what queer sense
Can this blob of matter be called a human being,
Whether Tithonus or Edgar L. Cummings.
I answer: in the *only* sense: he thinks,
He feels himself to be; a continent,
Lapped everywhere by our amniotic flood,
He contains the mystery of his mystery,
Is infinitely more important to himself
Than all the infinitely more important cosmos
He only senses over a few square inches.
All that he's lost was excrescence – desirable,
To see, hear, move, speak – but not essential;
You lose a nail – not YOU; your legs – a pity;
But YOU remain, clenched in the brittle skull.
Here fed with tubers, that's the only difference.

Take a crane-fly wandering in from the river,
Settling on a door you've sprayed with paint.
One leg goes, in the frenzy to escape
Two more – a wing – thick pencil scrawls
Grotesque millimetres away; now it knows
Not even God could separate paint from crane-fly
And leave enough of the latter. So it subsides,
Despairing. When you come along – my God, the paint! –
You expect it to welcome the tenderly offered rag,
The quick-crunch-and-it's-over. But no, it fights!
It tries to cringe. Not that it has any illusions
About ever getting away from this obscenity, it knows
The kindness of your gesture, but it just CAN'T
But try to protect its tiny brain from your pity.
Its little ego shrieks silently, LEAVE ME INTACT!
YOU DON'T KNOW HOW VITAL I AM.
Here, in this case, we've kept that ego intact.
I think I used the word excision,
As though what we cut *out* was expendable;
Call it rather a vast *amputation*
Of the body hacked clear away from the brain.
The *man* remains: meditates, desires, remembers.

Just to prove our point, watch now while Miss Wiggins
Stimulates a memory-cell. (Don't worry, he likes it;
Even when we happen to hit on a *bad* memory
He still enjoys the emotive exercise.)
Now.... Watch.... Keep one eye on the electro-
Encephalograph – WOOSH! See how the pencil goes
 - Boy! – shooting up and up in fantastic hieroglyphics;
We've obviously hit on something pretty big.
That cell-twitch we gave him means that he's now re-living
 - Down to the very colours, textures of garments –
A moment in his past: living it more *intensely*
Almost, in that memory-cell, than he did at the time.
A green coat *feels* itself slipping to the floor!
Maybe he's walking down a lane with his first girl,
Stepping carefully over a puddle, the scent of rain
Mixing with hers, while a blackberry branch whips

Across his leg, or maybe bending over a cot,
Yellow, with elephants pasted on it,
Where his son's fighting for breath against pneumonia.
Here's where the absence of speech, etcetera,
Proves a barrier. We never get through to him, or vice versa.
This memory is obviously emotional, but whether
Lust, anger, fear – your guess is as good as ours.
Our stubborn de-cipherers will wrestle with it
Seeking as always some clue to find the verbal
Equivalent, break the code. It's a helluva problem, *but* –
Sooner or later they'll do it.
The last twenty years, of course, haven't been exactly rich
In memories, except of his own thought-processes
(These violent scribbles certainly relate back to
an earlier period.)
                        How far, you ask, is he
Aware of his situation? Well, obviously
He *can't* be aware of it all, lacking
The normal apparati of discovery.
He only knows the contiguous bloodwarm
Solution, and our various probes – but this
Again is relative; aren't we, too, blissfully
Ignorant of our environment, outside
The (compared with infinity) contiguous
Galaxies a billion light-years away?
I admit the idea seems rather gruesome at first,
But he's happy because he himself exists.
'*Ay, but to die, and go we know not where!*'
That's something he'll NEVER have to experience.
I hope and believe he'd thank us – no, that's an under-
Statement – if he could,
And say moreover how proud he is being
Our proto-immortal, paving the way for ALL
To escape even three days' extinction. What a niche
In history! Why, may I end by making the outrageous
Suggestion that already our grateful Tithonus
Is gropingly beginning to sense
The presence somewhere *'out there'* of a Miss Wiggins,
As she bends over: *senses* the auburn angel

24

Who watched Prof. Joseph roll back the stone
Before the stone was needed? That may sound a crazy
Hypothesis; Dr. Reiner, our E.S.P. expert,
Reckons ten thousand years at least before
Our guest starts to develop his 'sixth sense',
But I've an idea this may be under-estimating
The powers of human adaptability.

Two Sonnets from Drifting Worlds:

LIMBO

The air-gauge clamped our heartbeats. When we searched
the cabin – firm again, relentless – a
stir of limbs confirmed the needle's lurch.
How full of charm proved our young stowaway!

How to tell someone that his offence is mortal
merely in that the fuel his weight would cost, the air
he breathes, is more than one frail cosmic-ship can spare?
His grin said, Company! Could not believe the portal

that leads to new worlds from this fetid womb
must suck him forth to – limbo. Yet he went
quietly into the airlock. There's no room
for sentiment in space. We meant

him well enough.   Zoë, it's not our fault; you must
eat. We bear supplies for the living, put them first.

A SYMBIOTIC PLANET

Stone gave way.... Too late! ... What seemed a mottled-green
puddle rose up to break George Meister's fall....

His eyes, that have grown stalks, can turn at will
inwards and see that distant blur, his brain.
That, and the spinal cord, and eyes, remain
of Meister; all else has been digested
or – in the case of clothing and gun – excreted.
He's now the steersman of the gelatine
disc: his old limbs' nerve-ends make it slither
along the dry river-bed towards some protein
prey it engulfs. They can make out together –
so one might as well adjust. No man should mourn
his fate, a change of circumstance, or count on
staying forever the same shape he was born.

Mercury

```
                              re-new'd
                       energy,            endlessly
                whirlingly               of your Lord's
                dazzled, and             passion,
        your flushed, fiery face         effulgence,
             so delicately,    PERIHELION   the splendour,
             like the moon,                so lost in
             librating, ever              like a caduceus,
                  as you                  us mortals
                  spin                    your charm works on
             Him-wards                    you must know
             -that even                   flective dancer,
             Copernicus,       SUN        perfect, unre-
        after a life spent                faster, and though, o
        studying orbits,                  flying faster,
        staring through                   his steps
        misty glasses                     to follow fitly
   at his local Palais,                   varying their mood
        regretted to his                  silvery heels
        clustered Poles                   quick
        (ere he slipped                   line,
             from us                      nigger's
        beyond recall)                    hook'd by the big
   never having seen                      rise,
   - o not your fam'd                     before you
             hermetically                 message,
   seal'd features, - but                 dawn a
             even the least   APHELION    later wakers and
             hermaion granted             giving us privileg'd
             some, of glimpsing           low blues,
                your blind buttocks,      a-sway in the
                     cool,     abandon'd,
```

28

S. F.

Apart from attacks by maenadic females, when
we called, under orders, on our Lemnos *omikron* colony
to investigate if the males are still infertile
as a result of fall-out from Lemnos *beta* (they are),
(See our SocReport, 'Gynocratic Neurosis');
an unexplained battery of meteors just before entering
the space-warp; a further attack by the six-legged
Protts of Arcton V, where we put in for re-fuelling,
(Caenius, a casualty, sorrowfully sun-cremated);
Iason all but engulfed by a giant crocus-like
'colchicon', after we had vaporized the rebel-
colonists' primitive death-ray; the expected
telepathic assaults by psi-birds, on re-approaching
our Galaxy – repelled by thought-screens; and mistaken
(it now seems) asylum granted a Colchian alien –
the voyage has been without incident,
its objective achieved – the World-Replicator recovered.
(TechReport: Mnemosyne Tapes a success in checking
space-boredom, but could selection of ArtMemories
be correlated more with crew's known sextypes?)

A Dead Planet

I

He captain primed his crew, disconsolate
Upon the bleak, the broken-pillared plain;

Waving a tentacle, he snapped. 'The State
Will want to know how primitive a brain

Presided here. We must *resuscitate*....'
(A thrill bestirred their pinions). 'We trust
                              the grain

Of skull that Luth is working on was late
Enough in time for the blueprints to remain,

Enabling our machine to build – and wait
To see what kind of animate was slain

So summarily, as it appears; what fate
Extinguished it.' Deep silence then.

II

        …The 'Man'
Such was the thing called, till the desolate
Decade of falling rain,

The white-hot ash – was shrivelled, bifurcate.
'Master!' his lips compounded while the skein

Was falling from the eyes he had just shut
On wife, on child: his faith was not in vain!

'Dear Christ! … how blissfully Thou dost abate
The grave's - ' His gaze took in the plain;

The ring of orbs devoid of love or hate,
The ray-guns poised to mow it down again

When they had sorted out its true estate.

Cygnus A

Removing hairgrips, nail-varnish, pensively brushing
Black hair down to the black
Bra, scattering a thick perfume on the night,
You've time to read me pointed texts
From the Gideons' Bible propped by the red-stained
    Kleenex
Till I must shut my eyes tight
While you slip
Off (still that ludicrous reserve)
Your diaphanous half slip.

But I prefer to gaze over the dark rooftops
And talk to you over my shoulder.
Somewhere out there, love, near-neighbour Rigel
Winks its white Chaucerian light
From Orion's heel; taking its petty flight
From the peaks of the Eagle
Burning through
Hitler. by Deneb and Altair,
Falls Vega's vulturous blue;

Cambering Perseus covers half the sky,
His spring from the weeping, huddled sisters,
To see if he can reach Andromeda
Before the formless monster lands—
Cassiopeia stretches out her hands;
And out there too's the glare
Of yellow Capella
And red, bull-eyed Aldebaran.
Yet since, sweet, all my stellar

Friends are in fact outshone and liquidated
By the sun streaming from the green shade
Suspended on this window over flickers of you,
I let myself go on and on
Past Deneb, into the dark breast of the Swan

Where only the radio-
Telescope,
Picking up its grating noises
Has any real hope

Of finding out that such a thing exists—
To a celestial catastrophe
Greater than most at various times enacted
In this Trust House — a cataclysm
Unforeseeable by their worst pessimism
— To two galaxies attracted
Into each other
At a slow thousand miles a second
Transformed to a smother

Which astronomers cannot untangle; Cygnus A.
…So girlish, now that your hollow mouth
has shed its lipstick flavour, you hold my hand
Preventively, I kiss black hair,
Your eyes shut tight in pseudo-tragic prayer,
Your weekend penates and
My cupidon
Clutter the bedside-table beside
The white text of St. John.

What must it be to have been born inside
Such a fantastic complication —
To pull aside a Cygnian tryst-house curtain
And watch the overwhelming merge
As whistling suns and planets all converge!
For a moment to feel uncertain
If one's discrete
Galaxy will ever emerge
With all its stars complete,

But *only* for a moment — the chances are
That not two single stars will get
Too entangled, as the run-through takes its course
In the next millennium; no glacial

Fate is ready, sweet, to quench an outer-spatial
Swan-light, though scores
Of spheres sail by
Each second —blues, golds and reds
In a greased, fabulous sky.

We're sure to see two 'silver plates' unpair
Round the Year of our Lord 90,000—
Though really, five hundred million years ago
These 'lovers' fled away, despite
Curiosity at Jodrell Bank tonight;
No doubt by this time snow
Has covered over
Many a planet, and Judgment-Day
Has heard the excuse of lovers:

"But that was in another galaxy,
And besides, the star is dead!"
While on live red-dwarfs, other will see St. John
Shine in your eyes, an aeon hence,
Recording, with their brilliant instruments,
That the red-shift heaven's undergone
So shyly, doesn't veil
Completely the Magellanic Cloud,
Though all space-trips fail.

Hera's Spring

'Nothing will be left of Jeserac but a galaxy of electrons frozen in the
heart of a crystal. I shall sleep, and without dreams. Then one day,
perhaps a hundred thousand years from now, I shall find myself in a
new body, meeting those who have chosen to be my guardians....
At first I will know nothing of Diaspar and will have no memories
of what I was before. Those memories will slowly return, at the end
of my infancy, and I will build upon them as I move forward into my
new cycle of existence.'

ARTHUR C. CLARK : *The City and the Stars*

Missing his noisy play around the
house, and remembering the time was no
doubt near, she hurried out, unkempt as
she was, and found him at last, pale-faced
and tearstained, hunched on the weir bank – no
fishing rod in sight – plunged in himself,
his pain. With a motherly tenderness
she wiped his eyes with her skirt-hem; she
knew; she gently questioned him; and said:

Believe me, dear, though it will seem strange
to you, I have wept too for all these
things you mention – and others that maybe have not yet started to haunt you
again. Do you recall, for instance,
the dark coppery flowers on the low
trees? The waterfalls, or methane-falls
- call them what you like – leaping off cliffs?
the strong, live winds, and violet sky
flashing with great clouds? And I expect
you have walked many a time with your
husband on those mountain-slopes as bright
as metal, with thunder laughing in
the ground, and clear red flame exploding
above you? I know *I* have – though with,
as it happens, a wife beside me

35

- a dear woman…. I too have been there,
Jeserac; a terribly long time
ago, but it's still precious to me.

Today isn't the time to convince
you that these eroded hills, blue sky,
green woods, not to mention the speckled
fish you like catching, are themselves not
unbeautiful … this first day, you've a
right to feel desperate. I recall
myself (though how many others in
between!) writhing in the ammonia-
snow I'd always thought of as home, and
was to again – tormented by the
globe your mind is filled with, shrieking at
my sisters to leave me in peace! Poor
mites, they ran off and told everyone
that a *yanu* was inside me! – This,
darling, was near Procyon, the light
your father taught you to find last night.

- Oh, don't think I don't understand; it's
the *beings* you gave yourself in love
to – not moons or cliffs! And the dull ache
of this you must expect never to
wholly leave you. How often one finds
oneself wondering – and the worst of it's
being completely unable to
share your dark thoughts with anyone else –
where is, say, Kersti? – a granddaughter
I once had somewhere in Boötes;
in which of the far-flung micro-files
of our cosmic city Diaspar
is that beloved pattern crystallized;
and where will she – or he – emerge again?
Yet one knows there can be no answer.
Only the dumb Selector knows that.

Still, it's the way of Hera's Spring; we
have to count our blessings. – I see *that*
too hasn't come back yet, dear! It would
soon, so I may as well remind you.
Ages and ages ago, on this
very planet (in re-emerging
here, we've come home, in the deepest sense),
men, who had previously 'died', as
though they were cattle or sheep, found out
the secret of immortality.
… Still doesn't bring it back? – Just *vaguely*!
Well, anyway, after they'd finished
rejoicing, they found that, after all,
the threatening shears were things they couldn't
do without. It's said the daffodils
withered in the poets' verses; nothing
seemed beautiful when nothing would pass
away! – in fact, they found the prospects
so deadly they clamoured for death to
be restored. Instead, their scientists
thought up a middle way, called *Hera's*

Spring, (I don't know who gave it that name).
But it came from the way Hera, 'queen
of the heavens' (you've heard of her in
this world) renewed her virginity,
that is her purity, each year, by
bathing in the spring of Canathos.
It fits. The spring we step into is
the frozen heart of a crystal, from
which we emerge, having just held our
breaths, maybe a million years later.

This first time is the worst, Jeserac
dear – your homesickness, if you like, is
focused, not radiated. When you
have had, like me, almost as many
parents alone as there are stars out
on these sharp, moonless nights – in fact, when

I look up, to whatever point in
the sky, I know I'll face a dozen
able to pierce through me, hazy or
bright, each with a dozen bereavements –
you'll find the ache is a thing you can't
do without either, in some queer way....
But here I am, talking as if I'm
antique, instead of being quite a
youngster in the city, not all that
much older or wiser than your small
brother Helderr, whose first world this
is! – and who, if I know anything,
has woken up howling for my milk
by this time! You stay here, Jeserac;
come home to us when you feel ready,
or hungry!

The Strait

'Duplicate self or friends; new humanoid plastic 2090 models,
guaranteed against all physical wear. From 7,000 dollars to our
15,000 dollar de luxe model.'

RAY BRADBURY : *Marionettes Inc.*

'Be sure you cable how this – chattel acts
in bed....' Caressed, her malice-lines dissolved.
'At least, for Christ's sake, order the De Luxe
model!' she jested through her rueful tears.

'I won't be cheaply copied!' Stretched across
a slim, fair arm that dived to find a banknote,
beat down his protest – 'He won't know his loss!'
Then, for one wild instant, she had solved

their bitter complex; he heard her throat
sing with excitement – why not endow the fool
with this ... android, and he take her instead?
Lulled by the pleasure-tapes tamped to his skull

day and night long, her loving dupe would get
all that he needed on a marionette,

and none the wiser! But he shook his head.
Rising in simmering wrath, she whipped
a gold robe round her nude bronze beauty, paced
out to the fresh veranda. He too slipped

from bed; stole after her; she faced
the garden's artificial insect-sounds;
her waist evaded him; he told her why
her plan would fail: 'we must remove the grounds

of rumour till it dies … this chance - ' He spent
his sorrowful rhetoric urging her that by
 - and only by – his flight could they prevent
the tell-tales' triumph. Together, were insane:

where, in the world, did he not have his spies?
And what could substitute for Yseult's eyes?

So, she must stay. Picture his lady now:
three months have passed. She lies here. Through
        the pane
full moonlight steeps – in no way different. Though
its bland eye bears one precious mote the more –

discarded garments on the coverlet.
Her diamond radio-earings drug her for
a time; then a sly, nubile marionette
mottles the screen within her, and alarm-

lights flash! Ah, Jealousy! Your swarms
of warheads, who can block them? Not
his blonde enchantment, whose self-accusations
strike worst: Why did she let him take this spot-

less model with him? – She could not compare
with it – with her! (Plucking a grey hair.)

It learns to satisfy; its eros-counter
records his mood, and flashes quick instruction
to kiss, to bite, play quarry or play hunter,
tells when to press, and when to use the light

moon-gravity to lose him for a while
coquettishly, a floating lunar sprite,
and when to plunge again … then, in the style
of Yseult, weeps when the long stillness falls.
40

And yet – and yet … he cannot breach these walls,
or even summon up the ram, unless
his labouring mind can desperately conceive
ingenuous Yseult in this expertise:

a ghostly rondeur nags its crescent charms –
earthlight, the Old Moon in the Young Moon's arms.

Space-ships are white to Yseult, dim reprieve;
are black to Yseult, soon or late eclipse:
Yseult ignores the founts where waters rush;
Yseult holds brackish water to parched lips.

Who pities Yseult, while she wishes it
melted in the lustful fire it feeds?
Who pities Yseult, yet could see her ash,
dead as that fire when her soul intercedes?

Yseult observes, with hollow eyes, the drear
darkness slow-tempered by a dreary grey;
Yseult sees sudden brilliant chromosphere,
red prominences, day cremating night:

Yseult puts on her jewels, as one locks
Yseult away, for safety, in its box.

Survive the heat, and then survive the cold.
Scrabble from fissures. The sky black all day,
Sun, earth and stars together casting bold
shadows and glares. Through dust, at a snail's pace;

find in a week maybe one crater that
yields scant reward for our labour. Back at Base,
only a fool would fling his gauntlet at
famished men whom the Mare Crisium

tortures and coarsens. Envying me, the crew
- as one man – howls for its soft white arms, pinches
its buttocks and plump breasts…. It's true,
her arms are white, whiter than Yseult's … some

flaw in the dye. Their needs are few; they'd not
be tortured by a ticking at its heart.

What virus spreads gangrene so swiftly, numbs
all organs? Base Camp dying. Oaths and stenches
thickly bandied. Only if she comes
with simples in her bosom will he live.

(Moon isolated; at Cape Kennedy
a medicorps groups.) Crawled back from the radio-hut,
he's now too weak to do anything but lie
gasping upon their bunk. It tries to give

him medicine, but he waves it off – 'Return
(he bids) when Yseult's signal comes through – wait
there, by the radio.' Its eyes burn.
He's seen these eyes before. Green froth has lined

his lips, he feels less rooted in the room,
and hears, far off, the silver rocket zoom.

'What, what could you have sacrificed that i
would not? What could you do? God! All the times
i've bathed his wounds from rockfalls, faced the wind
of plunging meteors with him, walked the rims

of craters – shared this world, such as it is!
Fought off their paws ... i say what more could you
have given him? Beauty? Yet i see now my
skin is fairer, features equal. No! –

when your morse threatened to help him, my knees
shook, I felt these walls we'd built here cry
out in protest, force me to invent
what made this plastic melt in fear – a lie.'

So Love made one Yseult divine, and made
one human. Blanched shores to a dry strait.

Elegy for an Android

At the last moment I
thought of the Neanderthals
pouring their flint arrows
into the rough grave
with its skins, haunch of meat, and
the wedding-ring I did
fling down onto your
casket was like a
lifebuoy, but where could I
possibly pretend that you were
going? I think that if I could
have paid more for you,
there would have been more persons
standing above that hole.

Bion and Theocritus
seeing your straight limbs,
classic grace of features and gold
dazzling curls would have
unhitched their pipes but
chancing to see the
tiny emblem 'made in
U.S.A' in the whorl of your
navel would have
shuddered and walked
on. Yet I loved you,
Vanessa, passing the love of
women.

Seeking a Suitable Donor

I can see now
               that last night
                        my heart
was beating and hammering packing-cases shut;
it had already left, in imagination;

I can see now
               that last night
                        my heart
lay sleepless in the almost bare, sleeping house
making an inventory of its joys and griefs;

I can see now
               the traffic-
                        warden's
change of expression as I drew up
at the first traffic-lights of the morning:

he knew me. I
               can see now
                        why the
newsvendor with the flapping poster, NEW TRANSPLANT
IMMINENT, raised his arm in triumphant

recognition.
               I can see,
                        now I
lie in this morgue, why I was hypnotised by
flashing lights, neon- and traffic-, and the just-waking lights
of the great Hospital of the Sacred Heart on my left
as I turned into the stream of the city-going traffic;

I can see now
                    why, though a
                              careful
driver, this morning I put my foot down hard,
and turned from my everyday route to tail the waiting siren

of the police-
                    car with its
                              twinkling
blue beacon. I can see now why a strange serenity
dispossessed my panic. There was nothing I could do,
I sought the surgeon as the leper sought Christ,
the evening newspapers were being rolled through the afternoon
                              presses.
It was written.
                    I watched my
                              body
borne in exultation through the city-streets jammed
with grey confused,
                    miracle-
                              hungry
commuters; I saw it cut from the living body and lifted high,
I saw that it
                    was red like
                              the still-
rising sun over the rows of suburban houses, in one
of which I had passed my existence; I saw
my wife lift the
                    telephone,
                              I saw
her murmur something, catch the wrong coat off the hook; I
                              saw
my heart rushed frozen, through corridors to a raised altar;
and I saw that I who had lived selfish and reserved

had been saving
                    myself for
                              this great
          giving; and I knew that all my hours

          have rushed towards
                    a red cross
                              given
          by strangers joyful in my death and

          resurrection.

Two Voices

The towel unstained.
By now, she realised, it had sailed
past the blood-islands, was rocking into a full sea. Storms
lashed it (hers), but still it survived, its
grotesque head stubbornly riding her
witchcraft. And love, too,
that intermittent pharos, lit it
on this journey to a lost father,
past her reefs and whirl-
pools. A following wind blew from her
dry coast. To aid it, to wreck it? She
fainted, in class. Her
friends, kind. She guessed they guessed. Tongues flayed
him. When, the vital spark? When the heart
pulses? Not murder
until. A snake or bird — no more. By
day she knit a coat each night unskeined.

Rubbing out half Orion, blood-islands hung in the black sky.
McAlister noticed it first. Puzzled, he lifted his
glasses. Called to the others. They came stumbling, clumsy
in their suits. They stared for a long time, incredulous.
What were they—the red islands, and the new bright star
a few degrees from Betelgeuse? Some new nova, maybe?
'My God! can't you see! It's Earth!'
Burkhardt cried, his words, his elegy, tailing into a sob.
'Damn it, you're right!' hissed Christesen. McAlister
was silent. Three men, magi, their hearts hammered at a small
globe's transfiguration. What could a man do but fix his thoughts on
the few heartbeats who had been his Earth? Each of them stood,
finally, in his good selfishness. Christesen, the farm in Wyoming;
McAlister, the house in Ohio; Burkhardt,
the apartment in Minnesota. Who can mourn a globe, a country,
a city, at once? Burkhardt knelt. The rest followed. Not
to pray, exactly, but to make the only gesture of defeat they knew.

Could simply watch as the violet-glow and the red ovals faded,
— chimerae, mirages — leaving the molten planet, drifting
west, now blotting Aldebaran. It was on time, still:
leashed to the sun. Fiery as at first. Then the rings
swung up, concealing.

The desert is happy, she mused — it
has so little, and it suffers so
much — but it's *happy!*
She walked without shoes, treading the grid
of the Arizona sand. Water
they can hoard for months,
so simple, to live on a shower,
grateful for the one cloud-smudge between
impermeable ultramarines.

Shells. Only the old
are here. Frenzied activity of
bowls and square-dancing and tricycling
after dinner. Trailer on trailer,
senior citizens,
flowery T-shirts and Bermuda
shorts, cherishing their shrunk or flaccid
limbs in the heat of the Phoenix. Less
alive than cactus-
limbs. Which, if you cut, yield water.
A lifetime's effort, husbandry, has
paid off in this late renaissance of
atrocious paintings.
Phoenix; a dying man deep-frozen,
stored. To await a cure. On a bus
she read this. Her eyes clenched shut. Where the
dying have so much
greed for life, how to kill you, child?

The chronometers that had stopped during that eternity of rending,
buckling, screaming metal, whirled bodies— they had sworn
a giant meteor-storm had hold of them, but the radar clear—
moved again…It felt as though they'd broken through some

crystal barrier a god had erected, to prevent the run-in
to Jupiter. 'What's happened?' asked Christesen, drawn, dry-mouthed,
finding a voice at last. 'Check all the readings.' The ship,
they found, had held. Only the sun's spectral analysis,
a minute but precise— but vertical—leap towards red, was different.
'Time-fault!' They stared at each other. Like men jumping over
ever-widening, ever-opening ice-cracks, they leapt from alternative
to alternative, but slipped at last, almost with relief, into the
abyss of Burkhardt's theory. 'How long?' McAlister asked;
'not that…it makes any difference, of course.' Burkhardt
studied the plates. 'Not long,' he said at last. '2000 —
3000 years —*Earth*-years.' (they could say the word now; for
many months it had stayed taboo, unrepeatable somehow,
like a dead primitive's name.) 'Not long… compared to the time-
slide of a million years Mount Palomar suspected when
gamma Boötis exploded. A mere hair-line fracture along the
time-dimension. But then, it wasn't a major explosion.'
—Irony skimmed over the tremors of shock. 'The biggest telescopes
in Andromeda won't even *see* it.' 'Then what happened to
our—? There was no need to finish McAlister's question.
The cabin silent with their grief's battering noises.

Her own flat solitude, nursing its
stealthy tiny enormous hateful
blessing —arteries cut through drought-land
to feed the secret
assembly of elements born in
a star's interior billions of
years ago —made her shudder when that
place of a lesser gestation in
a smaller desert,
'*Los Alamos*', hove up on the route-
signs —made her clutch her belly in fierce
possession. Later, her flesh browning,
two tarantulas' furry union,
a small sand-whipped furnace between rocks,
extermination
of lust, made her shiver again: fore-
taste, or memory? Once is enough
50

she thought, one thoughtless unscrupulous
finger. Once…

'Those cries we hear — Those burnt, flayed faces
—mirages. Like the red islands we saw bobbing about the sky.'
Burkhardt laughed, bleakly. 'They would simply have
—disappeared. The world exploded. The detonation triggered a
time-shift — an infinitesimal one, the crater reaching
beyond Jupiter, but not so far as Saturn — we being,
as it were, spectators staring numbly over the crater
yawning at our feet; our house —gone. One moment they
were there, the next—nothing: or rather, the scattered dust
they would be two or three thousand years on.
A comfort,' he said. ' A comfort. No-one suffered. No-one.
It was just like a film when a reel's been missed out
in the darkroom. No-one notices. The house is empty.
There is no-one to set up a hooting. Nobody suffered.'
Jupiter nearing, freefall held them, as in some immune
sterile indifferent glove a surgeon holds a hysterectomy.

One thoughtless unscrupulous finger…
She stood windowed at her hotel in
her slip for the heat, automobiles
honking towards pile-ups
and scrap-yards: shells on America's
mid-century littoral, (skyscrapers
ghosted by a puritan keel)… His
finger, too that sprang the ignition
behind closed garage
doors, was his final way of saying,
I never loved you. His head resting
on the wheel, his hands folded white
in his lap, a gesture of washing.
All I remember
is a phone-call. Except my high-school
teacher smoothing my back, for hours she
smoothed my back, till I calmed down. They were
bringing him home from New Jersey, then.

The third finger
I shall not know. But
it is coming. It will come as I
open my thighs for the second time
only, ever. The third crowing of
the male cock in my life.

Reaching for the
phone, girl in a
white slip, lifted above the knees with
the swell, on the seventh floor of the
Hotel Phoenix. She thought of the mice
who, crowded beyond endurance, crawl
up the sides of the cage, to die.

At rest, gathering strength, in the colonists' floating skin-city,
grown as large now as the country their ancestors came from.
'Naturally,' wrote Burkhardt to his journal, —for the shell of
Earth, for the dead eyes eagerly racing ahead of the paperknife —
'they do not believe they leapt out of a break in the film
some nine months ago, in the middle of a sentence or
a mouthful of wine, or asleep — they sleep endlessly
these people, most of the time we explore the city through
giant siestas, tiers of sleepers, their mouths twitching. They
regard it as something sad but remote, as legendary as
the loaves and fishes were to us. Something sad but something good,
for forcing the first pioneers to accept their exile here
on this globe of figs and honey. They have archives, they point out,
memories of childhood in their fathers' house, photos
of their fathers' fathers, a long line to the first crewcut.
It is useless to tell them that a gilled embryo
recalls the fish man has never been. The balloon-skin protects
them from curiosity, as from helium and hydrogen. They curl up
safe, undisturbed in their dream-world.'

Snowflakes crying against the pane and
sound of the automobile waking
me, in the early light. Struggling up
in bed, sense of dying, flying to
52

the window, fresh wheel-
tracks down the drive. It was myself took
those surprise trips to Philadelphia
or somewhere. The clinic. Recall a
wild little nose pressed to the elm-trees.
A stranger came, gave
me breakfast. If only they'd told me
my father was ill then maybe I'd
have understood. It was full of lies,
full of cruel lying silence, that house.

Child, he has not touched
me since. Are we spiders, mating so?
Since he will not come as a cloud but
as a Cloud, the mushroom dissolving
our egos, crucifying light of
the world, third cock, — yes, yes, try again,
ring the witch with the
transfiguring wand! The cigarette,
stubbed early, quivered. She lifted the
black phone. Engaged. Engaged. What other
mother, what other prophet? Her fists
beat enraged into the soaked pillow.

'My host abstracted tonight; he cannot settle to the colour-
symphony, the wallscreen of myriadchanging lights, his evenings
are filled with, when he swims up into awareness of
me. Normally, his fingers drum out the ever-modulating harmonies
as Picasso-like cubes deliquesce into halfcaught gothic grottos, kinesis
of shape and colour (to me), to him, pure sound, (his slightly-bulging
eyes are closed); "how perfect," he will sigh, "that pearl-green
dissonance! And how right that it can never be recaptured,
existing only for a second, not even that, not ever — destroyed
by beginning colours while I dreamt I heard it. The poignancy of art."
But tonight, fingers and voice are still; he shudders at sudden crimson
or purple chords. "Forgive me", he says at last, "I am not a good
host." His wife, he explains, has gone, Jackie has gone. I am
puzzled. No women went with the Jupiter exploration party. We
have seen none; we have seen only the artificial ova attached to

y-bearing sperms in the gestation centres. He smiles wanly. The
flick of a finger opens a case, that reveals tier upon tier of
shining white tables. "Jackie!" he explains, reverently. (His eyes are
flushed). "Today she left me. A quarrel. An infidelity." (His voice
trembling). "But tomorrow, or the next day, or the next" (his finger
lightly caressing one, then another, and another) "she will return.
Pain is good. We could not know joy without pain. But the
sculptors will not have programmed more than I can bear.
… A mescaline-base." Grown suddenly cheerful, he laughs at my
discomfort. "Peyote, flower of the desert, the Aztecs' ecstasy, the
Indian's consolation. One of the settlers, you remember, was of Navajo
blood."

The rain-mask they once fitted on a
dead child's face, now resting on the
pueblo altar, by the plumed sticks,
bowls of meal, and the wall-painting
of dark clouds above two plumed snakes, heads
raised, generating
lightning…*With your moccasins of dark
cloud, come to us*… Outside, swish of bare feet
through dust undampened for centuries.
Here, in the hardest country, last of
their kingdom, all prayers are raised for rain,
all heads, lifted, — even the head of
the child, even the
head of the child sacrificed prays
for rain, intercedes.

Needle-marks fading. Would not do that
now. Hurt him. Or drink that other. Still
the effects linger, time stops or runs
crazy, signs scream at my ears, insights
like x-rays see the
shadow in the future, —see you fight
for exit, bulleting your path, and,
as a hand reaches for ether, sees
you take the blast, before your mouth can
open to cry, shrink back, a cinder,
54

into the cave the fallout shelter
contaminated
from conceiving. Yes, it will choose *then,*
that instant…

the eyes of Christesen and McAlister glittered with feverish joy.
They had seen their wives again, held them, loved them. 'If anything
she's *more* beautiful,' Christesen exclaimed. 'These life-sculptors are
—incredible— so little to go on… a photograph — a few stumbling
memories — some taped dreams… Unbelievable likeness…'
'But they're not *real*!' For a moment the joy flickered,
their faces wincing as at a light blow from Burkhardt. ' In a few
days we shan't know that. Her arms are as comforting, she speaks of
our first walks together in Yellowstone, of the time a rattler scared
her as we were river-banking once, playing hooky from school. She's
real enough.' 'Man, it's *better* than reality.' McAlister burst in,
flushed. 'No sickness, and no bereavements. When I die,
May goes with me –no drifting out her life in a single room, dusting
ornaments, picking over old photographs wondering if it ever
                                                        happened.'
'What's real, anyway?' Christesen added. 'Did I ever rally *know*
Louise? I loved — and was bored with —a picture of her I created
in my own mind. Now, at least I love the Louise that's here —
he tapped the case swinging from his shoulder. 'Anyway,
just look at the alternatives. What are you going back *to*? They died,
they vanished, 2000 years ago — you know that! What's the point?
John, for god's sake, let them fix you up with — your family.'
Burkhardt remembered their words as the ship clibed through
the Jovian atmosphere. What *was* he going for? A sentiment,
                                                        —a blind need?
To find a daughter he'd never even seen! It *must* be a daughter…
It would be hard, on his own. Twice, his hand reached for the controls
to set it down: then checked. *I should have ordered them to come.*
They might have obeyed my rank still, habit dies hard. The white
colonial dwellings hazed into blue, featureless,— into a flickering
phosphorescent purple balloonshape… then New Long Island
vanished in the ammonia-clouds that battered the craft with storms,
focusing his thoughts, driving away all else.

The first flutter of your limbs,— feel! Tap
at the door, too frightened they were not
there, to knock loud enough to be heard.
Standing in that cold corridor, ghost
of the old nurse behind me, silent
oak-door in front, scared to make a move.
Every time I
was woken by an automobile
on the highway, and light was struggling
in, I'd leap out of bed and stumbling
over the cord of the red dressing-
gown I'd run down the corridor, my
heart hammering, and I'd stand outside
their room for hours,
trying if I could hear their breathing.
I'd tap — too lightly. What if there was
no answer, no scolding? No double
white hump in the bed, just a flat quilt?

Once or twice I did get close to him.
Remember when I ran home from school,
crying all over me, and called him
at his work… He dropped everything, drove
home. Put his arms round
me— for the first time, I think —told me
not to worry, —*they* were the lonely
ones, having to gang up, I was the
strong one, and was to be so always.
He talked very gently, till I found
I'd stopped crying. I'd forgotten that.

Sailing perilously through the asteroids' clashing rocks, descent
to the ochre planet, soul driven by its hungers to abide
pressures of a new gravity. Heart, liver and stomach
dragged down protesting into nature.
… A mixture of decay and fresh
life. Dust obliterated half-written reports in
the typewriters…Half-empty vodka-bottle…A game of
vingt-et-un, interrupted — playing the hand in session, Burkhardt
56

turned up a black knave, grimaced…Over a broad oak desk,
a full-length portrait of the Leader…Where he
touched, musingly, the index finger of the clenched fist, the canvas
gave, in a small flurry of dust. He shrugged his shoulders,
allowed himself a short, bitter smile. What killed the world,
— or was it someone else's— the world (I, John Burkhardt) kills…
Searching his brain to recall the plan the C.I.A.
procured of the Martian outpost, Burkhardt found at last
a stone flight of stairs, descending (it seemed) into the bowels
of the planet— in reality, down, he recalled, to the original
cave dwellings, turned by its later arrivals
into a labyrinth of fallout shelters.
The red ships undisturbed on their pads (and not even a Soviet
would have rushed so recklessly to their lethal home
or to the well-armed American moon colony), logic pointed
downwards for some relic of them. Burkhardt descended,
watching his step in darkness and unfamiliar gravity, the walls mossed.

Her friend's, her tutor's, voice, woken, came
through the night, across the continent,
soothing her agitation… 'Yes, he
did love you, your father probably
did love you; dying
was not a denial of this, it
was just that things had somehow got too
complicated to go on living…
Putting his arms around you was his
way, the only way he knew, maybe,
of telling you this,— begging you to
understand…' The voice, even as his
white teeth, sage as his
shock of white hair over the plump, sun-
burnt face, all of which came throbbing into the hotel room.

Yet even he,
did even he betray me? The night
he had us round for drinks…and we thought,
then, it had started, and were going

to get married, and were so happy…
But I slept, for a
couple of hours, on his sofa, and
when I woke up, they were in the bathroom, very close together, talking…
And I don't know what was said or done,
but he had changed, completely.

'So Light created man and woman, in a shelter full of
miraculous sounds and scents, the sweetest of roots and
funguses. But in time the shelter grew crowded with children,
who quarrelled over their rights. And some were sent to find
new shelters, not so good as the first but with plenty
of space for *their* children. Our forebears came here…'
Concentrating on his instructor's Slavonic dialect, Burkhardt
felt—heard—at the very last moment the slim naked shape slide
between them and plash her arms in the sightless stream…then a
shock of nausea as some obscenely clammy coil of life brushed past
him, imprisoned in her arms, as the child wriggled out again.
Chernov spat a command, and her footsteps padded into silence over
the rock-floor. 'Shelter-rat,' he explained, '— a delicacy. Excuse her
rudeness. Her family heard it swimming and sent her. Let's find
somewhere less exposed.' He took Burkhardt's arm and led him
confidently to a recess. 'To continue —they came here. And
shortly after, our first parents broke the only behest
Light had given them by making a stone image of Light Himself,
the unknowable, ineffable. Whereon he caused a devil,
Strontium, to spring from the head of the image and devour
the whole race. Except for those who had moved to other shelters.
Strontium sprang at these too, but Light had pity
on their terror and helplessness, and confined the devil in the first
shelter, now only fitted for him. But Light will not grant us to
hear Him again until — and in His own good time —
the hour of His last coming…That is what they believe.
The more intelligent regard it as a myth, of course: which is why
your story interests us. Your are not, obviously, a normal nomad,
there is this deafness in finding your way, these even more curious
(his hand fluttering to Burkhardt's face) mutations, where you
say you have a fifth sense. We are, we admit, puzzled
58

by your appearance here. But there are many, many questions:
we make nothing of a time-rift nor of this concept called darkness
that troubles you.'...A host of hands,
timid, awestruck, were groping for Burkhardt's face.

Questions and answers
at the Adoption Creche (her mother's
whim). *Question*: Do we encourage our
mothers to keep their babies? *Answer:*
No, since the sacrament of marriage
has been violated. The doctor
raped her with clean gloves,
sailing through the blown-up Alices,
brisk and late, a white
rabbit, every day the same, keeping
the queen waiting, fumbling his watch.

Your lips this
month shapes won't draw my nipples out or
any other girl's into giving.
An hour he did it, breaking down my
resistance, and his finger...the surge
a cliff wants to yield to, till even
the red warning-sign goes down in the
havoc of gorse and stone. Driftwood a
beachcomber picks up, somewhere, reads the
wave-scrubbed message, *Danger, Subsidence,*
tosses it on the
heap with the messages in bottles
from longdead shipwrecks, pair of sea-
boots, broken oar of a lifeboat.

And your eyes, this month opens , are to
see only these unlit aquarium walls,
though maybe one flash of light he'll
grant you as you get hooked out, darling.

Drifting in, and down, towards the tundra that was once Russia.
He set the controls towards the equator. America he could not face,

not yet, not yet. Over India, where the white cities still stood,
but lifeless. Then, out in the sapphire ocean, one flash of jade…
'Not from the moon…no. Before they abandoned their radios
they had already grown as narrow-visioned as the craters they
lived among, felt that life had been just too complicated
on Earth — hence the war, the bomb —so were becoming No-men
…better never to have loved, than to have loved and lost…
By this time they're probably no better than beasts.
But…Jupiter, now —we never made any contact through the
vapours. Maybe there's where you've come from. But no, why should
you lie? I've a man's judgement of your integrity, and more reliable,
my daughter's!…' — the girl's black eyes grew lidded, and a warmer
tinge mixed into the cheeks above the veil. '…Maybe I *have*
been here just nine months, however hard it is to take…' The
doctor's smile gleamed evenly, impishly, in his smooth mahogany
face, fierce sunlight flashed off his white robe, white hair. ' Excuse
our doubts, won't you? I myself think that you did come
from where you say, though such an expedition was never recorded,
but that for two thousand years the collective mind there
was in amnesia, from the explosion shock. Now, recovering,
the descendents re-live that race-memory of the Earth's trauma
as though it happened to them, personally. Your mind rationalises
this personal-collective confusion by assuming a time rift.
That's what *I* think. I must admit some of my colleagues, knowing
you less well, are more inclined to doubt your sanity!
Forgive them!' Three, they sat on the edge of the heat-veiled
sea, amidst iris and parsley, juniper and cedar,
on this one island of survival, circle of the sun.
Flat stones speed like dolphins from
Burkhardt's hand, his face pale beside the others',worn.

Slipping out at night, after hours,
up and down, up and down, boring the
square unlit avenues with questions,
watching the strange and thousandfold
replicated beast sprawled out in all
the house, its head in the front-rooms,
sipping beers, (lawnmowers tucked away,
through the drapes the one multicoloured
60

iris open still),
its privates in small enamel cells
scented with lavender. But those hours
were bearable, I could let myself
drift on the sky's spinning roulette-wheel,
deliciously drift —till they too stopped
— the sudden spring from the shadows — knife
or razor at my throat — garage-wall —
my breasts pumping, his hand fumbling —then
a car-door slammed and
he walked away, and I walked, my legs
jelly, and somehow I got inside
a house, blood on my coat, and there were
five boys playing cards, and I thought, God!
what have I come to? but they called the
police and my dean.

I could tell she didn't believe me.
Maybe she was right, maybe the blade
was back in my own purse. I don't know.
He just missed an artery. I search
in my purse for this coming Birth but
it's not there this time, I swear. I wish
to God I could find that bomb concealed
in my clothing, but I can't. The fall-
out triangles bloom
despite me.

They showed Burkhardt the laboratory where, in the centuries
after the trauma, after the year of waiting for the disease
in its wake, finishing all the survivors, to leap across
from the mainland, man had become ultra-human, had overcome
dying, using all his powers, all his science, all the divine
will coiled in the pit of his stomach. The room
was empty. A wide gash in the roof glassily refracted
bloodred sunlight into a pond where goldfish turned and turned
about beneath floating leaves. Beside the pond
      — the room's only furnishing — a prayer-mat,

where a youth sat crosslegged, his forehead pressed
to the ground.
Who does she see, looking down at him?
Not the child, and not the angel.
She's looking *through* him, as she must have
done all those months, looking through Joseph
or over his shoulder, at the lake,
where the nets were coming ashore, or
at the village street. Who *was* he? Some
Roman boy, taking fright at the first
alarm, re-posted
by a grinning officer to Gaul
or somewhere? Men. They stay together.

First false-pangs.   Nearer it came to her
time, she spent her days off from the light
work the Creche had found her, patrolling
the dense city streets or back and forth
impelled over the flowing bridge (by
the Evacuation Route sign), seeing
him in every turned
back; then, weary, in the gallery
where they had come to sketch. An hour she'd
sit before the 'Madonna of the
Eucharist' of Botticelli, while
menmoths fluttered to her hair's aureole
but reeled away as she stood up —burnt
by the smock her elder sister lent.

Deep in the cavern's recess, her tears fell (his head
in her lap felt their pressure), beginning to build
the stalactite of his everlasting absence (he who had
just arrived). This icy, translucent, irregular spear in
her memory would be his only epitaph. All her bribes
she tried, to keep him. 'Is she—so much lovelier than I?'
He smiled wrily. No. No, she wasn't. In any case she was
ash. She could not trouble herself about a woman who had
vanished two thousand years ago. No. Too often he felt
the naked skinny shade of a girl, clutching a shelter-rat,
62

wriggling past him. If he had never gone, would she have been
cutting circles in the ice in proud new skating boots,
grinning at him each time she came round? It was to answer that
question that he had to go, somewhere where death would give him
just the craziest chance of seeing his wife and his daughter
again. If he chose immortality, there was simply *no* chance,
'You've to return — just on the odd chances.'
When the plane lifted, before dawn, Boötes was setting,
Hercules, Libra and Leo were on the left. He set his course.

…Scales…and raw flesh being
weighed behind glass. *More! give her more of*
that?…I can see you but not touch you,
not hold you. To touch is bad for both.
Again! — take it off now, I want to
see it happen. There are too many
people in white coats here, too many
angels, everybody but the right.
Let my hands dig in-
to this straw and droppings, let my back
crack don't listen to me scream, now I
bear down and my muscles thrust for
me as they were taught, it is like I
learnt to ride a horse, twelve years old,
trembling not to do it badly not
to get shouted at, and he says nobody ever — ever — so well…and
my thighs tear apart
into a v and in the middle
of it a star, a gift out of the east, your
father and my father come at last,
—it grows —it grows— its parabola
jangling all the generals, too late, all
Early Warning Systems screaming and
at last, into my loins, into
my forgiving loins he strikes —, he lands —.

Ge

Note: in 1959, *a radio telescope was constructed at Green Bank, West Virginia, to listen for possible communications from other worlds.*

Crone-
goddess too soon, the natural
wild face Homer sang plastered with fly-
overs and cities and all the arts that disguise
barren age, she lives on her nerves – the mushroom
clouds of smoke are a cancer she can't give up. Mooning
and smoking, she drifts apathetically around her benighted
flat, its basement starkness lit by one naked lightbulb. Once
again her stale-sick odour reveals that her regular flow of war
is half-stanched in the tampon of a cause. Her milk, drying up;
her stomach distended from the sluttishly swinging negligee (she
has always spent her money on luxuries) is malnutrition not full-
ness. Call-girl, madam, for whom the phone has never rung, she
hungrily eyes the Green Bank receiver the owls swoop over for
now that angels, like dolls, have failed her, only a potent
stranger-god can cure her desperate soul. But a watched
phone never rings. He called maybe when she lay unconscious, or will try her unrecorded number at
random when the receiver hangs dead from
its wire and even the owls lie
on their backs.

The Head-Rape

Chastity veil: *Universal headdress, often highly*
ornamental, consisting of telepathy-blocks (usually
in the form of jewels) fixed to the critical points
of the skull (First used C.2800).
—from the Revised Anglamerican Dictionary

He raped her. Ripped the filaments from her skull.
She pleaded, by their home, their children, but
he tore the jewels off, mad with desire
to know her, to entirely penetrate,
like some Europa-storming bull.

A topaz —and he was in her in a flash;
he saw his bulging eyes leer down, smelt
the beastly courage he had drunk, he heard
blood pounding at her eardrums, felt
mind cleaving open as the stones

went…diamond —and he flinched at her
emotions …onyx
—and one hammer-thought —HE'LL KILL ME…
sapphire —and vestigial memory
rushed into him —a girl beneath her father,

on a blue quilt; with the more terrible
revelations of times she'd lifted jewels
willingly…which horned an urge to kill
in earnest this wombed softness he
screamed in; and since he had come nude,

and she could not help but see, he re-
re-felt his lust, being carboned in her brain,
sh re-re-felt the hysteria
that he re-felt, so he re-re-re-felt —.
Their bedroom infinite: two facing mirrors.

Blood and black hairs on the ripped veil.

Mr Black's Poems of Innocence

This sequence is a surrealistic exploration of the therapy of operant conditioning in mute schizophrenia, a therapy first revealed to the layman in a prize winning 1968 radio documentary, *Mr Blake*. *Mr. Black's Poems of Innocence* follows the line of treatment and terminology of the new therapy, but the case is fictional; Mr. Black and his operant conditioner are imaginary characters.

The 'poems' are envisaged as Mr. Black's reflections during his long silences or when he is back in the ward.

The eternal gates' terrific porter lifted the northern bar.
Thel enter'd in & saw the secrets of the land unknown.

Edited transcript by an operant conditioner of her treatment of Mr. Black.

Mr Black was found in a shocked condition, twenty years ago, and consigned to an asylum, where he was diagnosed as a mute schizophrenic. He has spent nearly all his time during those twenty years sitting on his bed without moving or speaking, and paying no attention to nurses or the other patients. At the time my treatment of him began, Mr. Black had no words at all.

On first entering the experimental room, Mr. Black ignored me completely, he might almost have been a corpse. I worked at gaining his attention by holding up objects, such as a pen or a comb and persuading him to say their names. The persuasion was by a very elementary form of reward and punishment; if he said anything that remotely approached the right sound, I smiled at him and encouraged him; if he refused to verbalize, I turned my head sharply and pretended he didn't exist.

INTERVIEWER: Mr. Black, I'm going to ask you some questions and I hope you will answer them. I would like that very much. Would you let me know your name?

MR. BLACK: (*no response*)

INTERVIEWER:	Where do you live? What is your address?
MR BLACK:	*(incoherent)*
INTERVIEWER:	How long have you been here, Mr.Black?
MR BLACK:	*(incoherent*
INTERVIEWER:	What's this, Mr.Black – in my hand?
MR BLACK:	*(no response)*
INTERVIEWER:	A pen. What's this?
MR BLACK:	*(no response)*
INTERVIEWER:	A comb. What's this, Mr.Black?
MR BLACK:	*(incoherent*
INTERVIEWER:	A handkerchief. Do you like snakes?
MR BLACK:	*(no response)*
INTERVIEWER:	Do you like pain, Mr.Black?
MR BLACK:	*(incoherent*

Thirty years ago I climbed up into this rooftop, maze of
    chimneys, after
My brother Robert. Grimes was a hard taskmaster. He came
    back drunk
Every night, and beat us. As I got higher and higher,
Scouring the blackness with my brush, I used to dream
Of breaking out of the slates, finding the sky hard with stars
And one small cloud sending down cool rain to wash my
    face free
Of the grime. Or of climbing down into some silken chamber
Where a girl like my mother would be sleeping in a wide bed,
Her bosom rising and falling and her long yellow curls
    spread out
On the counterpane. But I would always come back to my
    drunken master.
But that day, thirty years ago, I could not climb up or down.
This house must have been built on to, many times: a whole
Mineworking of twisting chimneys. I passed many small corpses,
Chalky bones gripping flu-brushes. In the end I too stuck,
My shoulders wedged between the sooty stone, no light
    anywhere.
I soon gave up struggling, it was pointless to shout. I have
    whiled
Away the years dreaming again the stories I used to read

over and over
At home, before Grimes caught me. I have grown a skeleton
Dreaming away the dark. Sometimes I think I heard the
        voice
Of the girl in the light, silken chamber. I struggle to shout,
But my mouth is full of black soot.

INTERVIEWER: *During the baseline measure, there was just
        silence or meaningless noises, what we term garbage or word-
        salad. Gradually however he began to show faint signs of
        interest, and to follow my hands.*
        Mr. Black, do you know what these are?
MR BLACK: *(no response)*
INTERVIEWER: Cup, Mr.Black. I'd like you to say CUP.
MR BLACK: *(garbage)*
INTERVIEWER: (coldly) That was garbage, Mr. Black. CUP
MR BLACK: *(garbage)*
INTERVIEWER: CUP! CUP! CUP! Mr. Black, CUP.
MR BLACK: Ka, Ka.
INTERVIEWER: GOOod! Now CUP.
MR BLACK: *(garbage)*
INTERVIEWER: C'mon now, Mr. Black. CUP.
MR BLACK: Ka, ka.
INTERVIEWER: Good. That was nice, you know that? CUP.
MR BLACK: Cu-
INTERVIEWER: GOOod! Mavellous. I liked that, I really did
        like that. Now try again. CUP.
MR BLACK: Cup.
INTERVIEWER: GOOod BOOoy! That was VERY GOOD. That
        was really something. Cup.
MR BLACK: Ka, Ka.
INTERVIEWER: Good. Cup.
MR BLACK: *(garbage)*
INTERVIEWER: (coldly) That was garbage, Mr. Black. CUP. CUP.

I follow the trail of the lost seekers, Alan Quatermain the
        great hunter,
Stout Curtis and brave good Sir Henry Good; in my hand
The torn yellow parchment bequeathed by the dying Portugese
68

Seeker, Da Silvestra, to later seekers; crawl with it in hand
Over the shimmering desert fiery gold under a round red sun
Filling half the sky and about to explode; suddenly, on the
    horizon,
Out of nothing – Sheba's Breasts, each berg fifteen thousand
    feet
In height, linked by a sheer rock-cliff, swathed in cloud-mists
Like a woman asleep, veiled; extinct volcanos, they are gold
In the throbbing sunlight, except that they rise into snow-
    nipples.
Miles to go yet – but there, a dozen yards away, half-sunk in
    a koppie,
As the old Dom's map predicted, unsuspected, the pan of
    bad water.
But as I scrabble to it and stoop to suck, it slips away from me
Like the lips of a harlot, in loathing, turned aside, spitting
Saying, is it not enough you burrow into my hole
My diamond-mine, my lineaments of scrofulous apathy?
    Across
The desert, I climb the foothills, following the crushed
    twigs
Following the three pairs of footprints still preserved
In the snows after a thousand years and I enter a region of
    ice and silence,
The air thin, difficult to drag your feet;
But at the crest, a cave, and I enter its darkness,
And there, at the end of the cave, seated on a ledge as expected,
Is the body of a man, Da Silvestra, the yellow skin – still
Preserved by the cold after two thousand years – stretched tight
Over his bones; in middle life, his features aquiline,
The remains of a woollen pair of hose, a yellow crucifix round
    his neck,
Naked else; a small bone pen at his feet, a wound in his arm
Where he had drawn the ink; now all his words have flowed
Into the winds and mists that swirl around Sheba's nipple.
His mouth hanging open, head slumped, the maker of the map
    has nothing to say.

INTERVIEWER: MR. BLACK!! LOOK AT ME!! CUP! Mr.
    Black. CUP!
    (he had this way of, you know, going dead on you, you might
    have been a wall for all he knew or cared, and when this hap-
    pened, I'd shout his name, real loud, and as though I was mad
    as hell with him. It was a kind of electric shock, and it did seem
    to work, he did seem to come just a little out of his trance.
MR BLACK: *(garbage)*
INTERVIEWER: NO! Mr. Black. NO! NO! NO! Say no, Mr.
    Black.
MR BLACK: *(garbage)*
INTERVIEWER: No. No. C'mon now, I thought you said it then.
    No.
MR BLACK: No.
INTERVIEWER: (caressingly) BEAUTIFUL. That was terrific.
    That was so nice. No. No.
MR BLACK: No.
INTERVIEWER: GOOod! You make me happy the way you say
    that... Do you like food?
MR BLACK: *(no response)*
INTERVIEWER: Okay Mr. Black, you've been working very hard,
    you've been really trying, I'm going to let you be taken back to
    the ward now.

It has been restful here; knowing I was in a vice,
I could forget his surliness, and dream of the stars and the girl,
Quietly. But now that skin and flesh have dropped away
        from me,
I find that I can move my shoulders down, and there is my
        mother's
Voice calling. I don't want to climb down. My limbs are
        stiffly cramped
But her nipples call. Her white hands will wash me clean
With a heavy sponge. And I will wriggle into her bed.

INTERVIEWER: What's this I've got between my fingers, Mr.
    Black?
MR BLACK: *(no response)*
INTERVIEWER: Cigarette. Say cigarette.
70

MR BLACK: *(garbage)*
INTERVIEWER: CIGARETTE.
MR BLACK: *(garbage)*
INTERVIEWER: That was mush, Mr. Black, that was garbage.
    CIGARETTE.
MR BLACK: Sa, Sa.
INTERVIEWER: GOOod! Now again, Mr. Black. Cigarette.
MR BLACK: Cigarette.
INTERVIEWER: MARvellous! It really was. I'd like to give you a
    puff for saying that, Mr. Black. Once more and you can take
    it from me. Cigarette. Cigarette.
MR BLACK: *(garbage)*
INTERVIEWER: CIGARETTE.
MR BLACK: *(no response)*
INTERVIEWER: MR. BLACK! Look at my hand! MR. BLACK!
MR BLACK: *(garbage)*
INTERVIEWER: CIGARETTE.
MR BLACK: Cigarette.
INTERVIEWER: GOOod BOOoy! Do you want to take it from
    me, Mr. Black?

Behold, in the dark, a man.
A yellow crucifix.
Middle-height, middle-span;
His limbs dry as sticks.

Though natives swear
His body to glory ascended,
The Dom is here;
Here his journey ended.

A wound in his arm
Where the great map spilled;
Now he sits dumb
His voice is stilled.

Forty days he survived
The tortures of the desert;

On snake-flesh he lived,
And wrote with bone his chart.

With what courage he rose!
But himself he could not save;
See how his vision froze
To a ledge in a cave.

INTERVIEWER: It's a bit cool today, Mr. Black, do you want a
    nice drink? Say tea and I'll give you some.
MR BLACK: *(garbage)*
INTERVIEWER: Tea, Mr. Black, and I'll pour you some.
MR BLACK: Tea.
INTERVIEWER: Lovely. Really nice. Tea
MR BLACK: *(garbage)*
INTERVIEWER: No, Mr. Black. Tea
MR BLACK: Tea.
INTERVIEWER: GOOod. Tea and you can have some.
MR BLACK: Tea.
INTERVIEWER: LOVEly. Terrific. Tea.
MR BLACK: *(garbage)*
INTERVIEWER: TEA.
MR BLACK: Tea.
INTERVIEWER: GOOD, very good. Tea.
MR BLACK: *(garbage)*
INTERVIEWER (coldly) That was garbage, Mr. Black. Tea. Tea,
    and I'll give you some.

You are more beautiful than in any of the pictures rising,
Your sweet smiling face framed by the long yellow ringleted hair,
Arms stretched out to clasp me to the bosom of your nightgown.
You offer me the keys to the gates, all your body's openings.
But I cower back into the fireplace, your breasts have turned
Into gourds of gold. On your forehead a rose
Is being gnawed by a grey worm. How can I warn you?
My mouth is dry.

INTERVIEWER: MR. BLACK!! THIS WAY, MR. BLACK!!
..That's right. Okay, (*he's not interested in the tea*) let's try
some candy. Do you want to say candy and I'll give you some?
MR BLACK: *(garbage)*
INTERVIEWER: Candy. Candy.
MR BLACK: *(garbage)*
INTERVIEWER: C'mon now, kid. Candy. Say candy.
MR BLACK: Ka, ka.
INTERVIEWER: GOOod. Candy
MR BLACK: Ka, ka.
INTERVIEWER: Candy. Candy.
MR BLACK: Candy.
INTERVIEWER: (rapturously) TerrRIFic! Good talking. I'd like
to give you a square of chocolate for saying it so nicely, Mr.
Black. Candy. Candy.
MR BLACK: *(garbage)*
INTERVIEWER: (coldly) No, Mr. Black, that was word-salad.
Candy.
MR BLACK: Candy.
INTERVIEWER: (rapturously) GOOod, Marvellous. That was a
honey. Candy.
MR BLACK: Candy.
INTERVIEWER: GOOod! Real nice. You've come a long way
today, Mr. Black.

The ghosts of Quatermain, Curtis and Good tell me that when
     you reached
The top of the mountain and could climb no further, the
     voice you heard
On the plain could be heard no more, there was only the
     shrieking wind
Around Sheba's barren nipple, grey clouds scudding, letting
     through
Streaks of the dying sun. They tell me you washed
Your sand-raw wounds in the snow. Then you dismissed
Your bearers. Looking down at the other side,
You cried gently. Then found yourself this cave, sat down and
     there
Eased yourself of thirty years' saintliness in a thin stream

Of milk. We see the grey stain on the floor still. There was
No thunder striking you, only a soft down-flurry of snow across
The cave-mouth from the peak of the nipple. I reach down and
    break
The string of the crucifix.

INTERVIEWER: *This is Friday, March 3rd, session 5. Mr. Black*
    has been doing a lot of vocalizing, he's been chatting at quite a
    high rate. Of course it's mixed up with a lot of garbage. We are
    looking at a picture of a horse.
    Okay, Mr. Black, let's look at the picture. What's this, huh?
MR BLACK: *(garbage)*
INTERVIEWER: A horse. Horse. Horse. Horse. Horse. I'd like
    you to say horse.
MR BLACK: *(no response)*
INTERVIEWER: *I broke off recording there. We didn't get any-*
    where for, oh, five minutes. Then it started moving.
MR BLACK: Horse.
INTERVIEWER: GOOod, Mr. Black. Yes! Lovely talking.
    What's this?
MR BLACK: H - h –
INTERVIEWER: Yes, horse. What's this? Horse.
MR BLACK: Yes
INTERVIEWER: OH! GOOod, Mr. Black. Yes! Lovely talking.
    What's this?
MR BLACK: *(garbage)*
INTERVIEWER: Point to the horse, Jimmy.

I go down into the secret land that Solomon ruled;
A place of paradisal mills each one a thousand storeys high,
Light walled in glass, wheel within wheel and without wheel
    visible,
To the amazed eye; they stretch away to the horizon,
The low hills that lead to other mills,
And above the mills of industry where metallic slaves toil,
In a billion glass compartments the Greys are resting,
On the eve of some great battle, for their faces are savage and
    composed;

I see them eat, make love, with the air of dream
As men do before a battle, a million raise glasses of milk to
    their lips,
A million urinate; I see none born, none dying;
All are in the prime of manhood, womanhood, all handsome,
    all indistinguishable;
And as I watch the magnificent regiment of the Greys at rest
Before certain annihilation, waiting with a calm despair,
It seems to me that Death has already touched them;
Though below, out of the shining mills, a constant stream
    appears
Of bodily organs; of hearts, lungs, kidneys, genitals, and brains.
It is the last, epic stand of the Greys.

INTERVIEWER: MR. BLACK!! MR. BLACK!! FOLLOW MY
    FINGER, MR. BLACK! What do you see, Mr. Black? Huh?
MR BLACK: Horse.
INTERVIEWER: GOOD BOY! That's good talking. Now what's
    this in my hand?
MR BLACK: Chocolate.
INTERVIEWER: Chocolate, that's nice. You may take it. You
    named it correctly so you can have it. Now what's this?
    Brooch. Brooch.
MR BLACK: (*garbage*)
INTERVIEWER: Give me the chocolate, Mr. Black. What's this?
MR BLACK: Brooch.
INTERVIEWER: GOOod! Good talking, Jimmy. Very good.
    That's a nice chocolate. You may eat it for talking so nicely.
    Now, Mr. Black, would you tell me, what is this? What is this?
MR BLACK: (*no response*)
INTERVIEWER: (anger) Back to the ward, back to the ward. You
    don't know. Out! Out!

Your voice is all caresses; even your scoldings are part of your
    love,
As when I skipped off the pavement or would not drink my
    milk up.
You send me to bed but creep up to kiss me.

You laugh, pulling your nightdress over your head, and I long
To reach out and embrace your loins or vanish into that dusky
Grove. But everywhere I touch finds gold not flesh;
Spreads over the serene pacific to the musky indentation,
    spiced,
Trickling down the line of childbirth I printed in you
To the vast jungles of Africa, lakes and cascades and rivers
Shrivelling as the pores close under liquid gold. Your hair
Brushing against me now is metallic, bleeds my face.
The worm's chaps gnaw and you do not seem aware. Your
    laughter,
Golden and metallic, swarms through the rooftops and stirs
All the small skeletons into limb-jerkings. Like insects lying
On their backs, they strive for the word which pleases you.

INTERVIEWER: *It's teatime and I'm going to give him some tea.*
    Mr. Black, what's this?
MR BLACK: Bread.
INTERVIEWER: You're right, it's bread.
    I love you talking. What's this, Mr. Black?
MR BLACK   (*garbage*)
INTERVIEWER: That's chatting, Mr. Black, what's this?
MR BLACK: Butter.
INTERVIEWER: GOOod! That was good. Yes, butter. What's
    this?
MR BLACK: (*garbage*)
INTERVIEWER: Milk, Mr. Black. Say milk and I'll pour you a
    glass.
MR BLACK: (*garbage*)
INTERVIEWER: Nice chatting. Milk.

Grey, behind crystal-walls
The Greys are resting;
Flower of Kukuanaland.
And all, the same arresting
Tomorrow appals.

Awaiting the mighty war
That may never come.
76

How long must they wait to hear
The cleansing drum,
The cosmic roar?

A million urinate;
A million drink;
A million stare at screens;
A million think;
A million masturbate;
A million cry but keep
Tears hidden by a hand;
In a nightmare twitched
By the Grey's last stand
A million million sleep.

God's bravest, combat-steeled;
But how if they never hear
The exultant warcry *Koom*!
The thunder of spear on spear
Tapping against shield?

INTERVIEWER: *So far today we've had an enormous amount of verbalization, but very few audible words. Also one of his cadaver-like withdrawals in which he just stared down at his hands. But then came a truly amazing sequence of positive responses. We were looking through some more pictures...*
Okay, Mr. Black , what's this?

MR BLACK: Car.

INTERVIEWER: Car, GOOod. That's nice. And this? Can you say this?

MR BLACK: No.

INTERVIEWER: Tape-recorder.

MR BLACK: Tape-recorder.

INTERVIEWER: Oh, Mr. Black that's a honey. And what's this?

MR BLACK: Traffic-lights.

INTERVIEWER: Oh my gosh! (*laughter*) This is terrific Mr.
Black. (*I've never had to feed him so fast – about every other time.*)
What's this? – Oh, I'm sorry, I've spilt some on you.

MR BLACK: Spilt, yes.
INTERVIEWER: MY! (*laughter*) I can't believe you're talking
    so well, Mr. Black. What's this?
MR BLACK: Aeroplane.
INTERVIEWER: What are these?
MR BLACK: (*no response*)
INTERVIEWER: What are these, Mr. Black?
MR BLACK: Skyscrapers.
INTERVIEWER: GOOod. What's this?
MR BLACK: (*garbage*)
INTERVIEWER: Can you say typewriter?
MR BLACK: Typewriter, yes.
INTERVIEWER: Beautiful. What's this?
MR BLACK: Bridge.
INTERVIEWER: Good. Oh you're working terrifically, Mr. Black.
    I can't remember when I had so much fun.
    And so it went on, you just couldn't stop him, he just wouldn't
    be inappropriate! And when he finally flunked out – I think
    he was tired too – I was actually relieved! I was so tired, he'd
    really worn me out, but all the same I felt good, I felt that I'd
    really started to break through.

Sheba, your trillion eyes are glazed and reflect the sun.
There is no warmth, no promise in them except the harlot's
    promise.
Yet your eyes shone once with maidenlove in a face that
    was fertile.
To the farthest low hills loped by the zebra. Now they are tiers
    of gold
Sunken in a dust-bowl.

INTERVIEWER: *For the past month, I've been attempting to re-*
    instate his reading and writing behaviour. So far he's learnt
    how to read one word at a time.
    I'd like you to read this for me, Mr. Black. Read this.
MR BLACK: (tonelessly) The red balloon.
INTERVIEWER: GOOD. VERY good. The red balloon. I like you
    reading to me. Read this.
MR BLACK: (*garbage*)
78

INTERVIEWER: That was garbage, Mr. Black. I turn away my head when you say that. There was…
MR BLACK: There was…
INTERVIEWER: GOOD. There was a red balloon.
MR BLACK: Balloon, yes.
INTERVIEWER: Good. There was a red balloon. Now tell me what colour was the balloon, Mr. Black?
MR BLACK: Red, yes.
INTERVIEWER: Very good. Red, yes. You're working beautifully. Right, let's read this, shall we?
MR BLACK: There was a red balloon.
INTERVIEWER: TerRIFic. Oh, I liked that. Now, can you say the whole sentence for me again, Mr. Black?
MR BLACK: (*no response*)
INTERVIEWER: C'mon Jimmy. There was a red balloon.

Sometimes the Greys swarm out on to the streets, form up
    in phalanxes
And look up at the sky. A dusty breeze cuts across the blue
And a shadow falls as the sun is darkly eaten. A soft murmur
    rises
As the red globe is extinguished they remember the stranger
Who was able to darken it at will, and they wait for him again
To step down from the sky; but the darkness passes and the
    murmur
Fades as the breeze, the streets are empty.

INTERVIEWER: MR. BLACK!! LOOK AT ME, MR.
BLACK!! Okay, Mr. Black. Let's try you with some food.
New behaviours were starting in Mr. Black's life generally, as a consequence of his new verbal behaviour. He walks around, and dresses and undresses himself. I'm actually watching him shave right now – we brought a bowl and a mirror into the experimental room – and I'm giving him encouragement, re-inforcing his behaviour with food.
Now, Mr. Black, you're putting on shaving-soap, aren't you?
MR BLACK: Shaving-soap, yes.
INTERVIEWER: That's good. And now you're making a lather.
MR BLACK: Making a lather.

INTERVIEWER: VERY good. And this morning we made the
    toast and the tea together, didn't we? And now what are you
    using, Mr. Black?
MR BLACK: Razor, yes.
INTERVIEWER: Oh that's lovely, I'll have to give you some fish
    for saying that. As soon as you've shaved we'll have some lunch.
    Do you like fish?
MR BLACK: Want some fish, yes.
INTERVIEWER: Oh my gosh, yes! And maybe you'd like some
    potato and beans?
MR BLACK: (*garbage*)
INTERVIEWER: That was garbage. I turn away my head.

There on the ground where the stone has risen are the crushed
Bones of old Gagool and near them the poor decaying body
Of Foulata who died peacefully in honest Good's arms for the
    sun
Cannot mate with the darkness nor the white with the black
But O her soul is white. Da Silvestra on the mountain
And Foulata in the depths – what hope is there
That we can survive? No need to mourn the queen and king
When I too am walled in the living grave. Leaving the boxes of
    diamonds
As all seekers have done I heave at the stone-ring
In the floor, and descend, following the draught of air
Into a maze of mine-addits deep in the mountainside, the
    tricklings
Of a stream propelled from nowhere to nowhere; I too
From nowhere to nowhere through the winding chimneys past
    many a
Trapped skeleton, but at last a pinpoint of light, light only to
    those
In pitch darkness, and I crawl forward forcing my shoulders
    through rock
After rock through earth ever narrower till I am through with
    a heave
The jackal-hole and rolling over and over uncontrollably
Down the mountain slope. And the dawn bursts to show

Around me and under me, the bones of beasts strewn on the
hidden snow.

INTERVIEWER: *This is the last session. With the aid of cue-cards,*
we have been working on questions which might be useful to
him in the ward. I'm going to cover up the cue-cards and see
what happens.
Mr. Black, ask me a question about the month.
MR BLACK: The month.
INTERVIEWER: Good. Ask me a question about the month.
MR BLACK: (tonelessly) What is the month?
INTERVIEWER: Good. It's August – that's nice. Ask me a question
about the time.
MR BLACK: What is the time?
INTERVIEWER: Good. It's – it's after eleven. Good. Question me
about the day.
MR BLACK: (garbage)
INTERVIEWER: Question me about the day, Mr. Black.
MR BLACK: What's the day?
INTERVIEWER: It's Monday. That was very good. Ask me a
question about the ward.
MR BLACK: What's the ward?
INTERVIEWER: Good. It's Cedar Ward. Ask me a question about
the doctor.
MR BLACK: (*no response*)

A few slow beasts still crawl
Through the flattened undergrowth,
The jungle carved by the flight
To a fireball's aftermath.

The rest in their myriads crushed
On the snowy mountainside,
Look back at the scene they had left,
And their clamour died.

Famine settled their limbs,
The night shone icy and calm;

The deer lay down by the leopard,
The lion covered the lamb.

INTERVIEWER: *Now we're just going to talk generally for a while.*
Do you like these flowers, Mr. Black?
MR BLACK: Nice flowers, yes.
INTERVIEWER: Good. They are nice. I picked them myself in
the garden this morning. It's late for them but they're so lovely.
Is it nice today?
MR BLACK: Today.
INTERVIEWER: Is it nice weather today?
MR BLACK: Lovely weather, yes.
INTERVIEWER: Good. It's lovely weather, very sunny. What
colour is my dress?
MR BLACK: *(garbage)*
INTERVIEWER: No, what colour is my dress?
MR BLACK: White, nice.
INTERVIEWER: Oh, good. I'll have to give you some candy for
doing so well. Oh gosh! it must be very stuffy in here, Mr.
Black, I'm sorry. What have I just done?
MR BLACK: Yawned, yes.
INTERVIEWER: GOOod, I yawned. That's very good.
*The treatment was completed, and it only remained to take the
final baseline measures.*
What is your name?
MR BLACK: Black, yes.
INTERVIEWER: Where do you live?
MR BLACK: Maple Ward.
INTERVIEWER: How long have you been here?
MR BLACK: *(garbage)*
INTERVIEWER: How long have you been here?
MR BLACK: Twenty years.
INTERVIEWER: What's this?
MR BLACK: Pen
INTERVIEWER: What's this?
MR BLACK: Comb, yes.
INTERVIEWER: What's this?

MR BLACK: Handkerchief.
INTERVIEWER: Do you like snakes?
MR BLACK: No.
INTERVIEWER: Do you like pain?
MR BLACK: (*no response*)

While she sighs in her sleep
His lust devours,
Lip under velvet lip,
The red raw flower.
When she wakes up,
Warm in her rumpled clothes,
She yawns, and has no mirror
To see the rose.

INTERVIEWER: *When I went back to visit him three months later
I found that, though there had been some regression in his behaviour,
he could still respond positively. I also learned something that
touched me very deeply. About a month after the termination
of treatment, one day he just disappeared. He'd just walked
out of the gates and kept on walking. I guess deep in his
mind he wanted to walk home. He walked all that night. The
next day a charge nurse found him and he was brought back.
When I heard about this, I didn't know whether to be glad or
sorry. He might have got himself killed, of course, he really
wasn't safe, and yet I think I was really glad. It showed that
Mr. Black was alive again, or coming alive, and he'd been dead
a long time.*

You tempted me with your loveliness but you withdrew it again;
When your legs were stretched wide and your arms, I saw that
     your last
Extremities, arctic and Antarctic, were also imprisoned in gold.
The last pore shut fast, you could breathe no more. I waited
     for you
To speak, but you did not. You have destroyed me with absence
—death. Now I walk through you to find you, heal you of
     dumbness;
Or all shall say, without a use this shining woman lived,

Or did she only live to be at death the food of worms? If I
Can find one pore of your body not wholly dead and open it,
And plant therein one seed, one flower... you will come to me
     again
And speak to me. Through Highgate and Hampstead, to
     Poplar and Bow,
To Islington, all night I walk – home, home.
Dawn breaks over the Surrey Hills. And behind me I see
An angel, smiling, holding out his hands in blessing,
Quickening his steps to catch me up to guide me on my way
To save you, bring you back.

Computer 70:

Dreams & Lovepoems

she is pleased   excited by the handsome powerful and older man
who drives   masculine and arrogant   with as firm a skill
and watchful care as though   it might be   a thousand minuteman
warheads couched in their steel burrows   obedient   to the will
of his left hand   guiding and adjusting   and
the closed air full of the song   of suave flesh
wined under smooth party dress   his right hand
hovering over complicitly tensioned synchromesh
the windscreen   framed the night   a radar screen
where only innocent objects   and familiar   flashed
roadsign   a dead hedgehog   trees   a risen moon
but risen nothing that could   perturb   he clashed
gears tyres and brakes   turned right   an arrowing road the springs
rode easily   catlights   disappeared   she feline settled   a ridge
they leapt   drenched in excitement   her scented   underthings
flesh steel upholstery   talk   one rocket-head   a bridge
reared up   she drowned   in her surrender to the waiting dunes
she had no answer to   nor failsafe   to the embrace   beneath
isolating intimating   night   she was the undine moon's
penetrable hymen   she sought a star   a breath

85

1

Your thighs meshed in the glow
of the instrument panel,
a gravitational field
drawing eye and hand;
intransigent flow
of digits, mile on mile;
man in the dead of the moon
tonight; hedgehog dead on the road,
flesh whirled on michelin;
images that time
alone must reconcile.

who is this lady dawnembarking at gravesend so belle and blanche the mast-
lights of a passing merchantman glided behind and through   her gloved
hand given to the poet muffled   & gasping for breath   *she will not last
the voyage* he confided   *he is more ill than I*   she whispered   moved
against his heart he carried a stone   cornelian
heavy and cold as the lightyears he would spend
unpillowed   on the breasts   of Fanny Brawne
now the lady belle and blanche   at gravesend
rises to accompany endymion his last autumn moon voyage becalmed
in each breath's painful   hopeful channel   he watched his actual
migration glassed in her hatches wide her blood seethed   slammed
in storms he fainted   scarcebreathed   its meaning   he could not fail
she is the wake   his name   will slide
into   the chaos of unwritten poems
Fanny   that still   unravished bride
came Lulworth & a lull   gleams
by *Maria Crowther*'s   anchorage   a star
the lady   unsupported   can barely stand
consumed by   themselves   all they are
they walk   the dark sand   stone in hand

2

Dying, she is not also
well
today: an extra pallor.
Delicately
from tree of ovaries, tree of lungs,
bloodleaves fall
into soft linen.
So like my mother.
I pun savagely
for her. She presses upon me
painfully. The ship that bears
me is *Maria Crowther*,
woman.

If I had not
grown cold at the last, (you said),
the figures on the urn had lost
all that they hold, withhold.

Swallows gather but they will return.
Already your face is hard for me to compose.
Your lock of hair; your white cornelian stone.

From the first kiss, all is clear:
Severn will sketch the death's head, to keep awake.
And I shall hold the stone,
cornelian.

Already with thee
the night is tender.
Who?

Could I but dream
this girl was you,
I should get well,
I should return.

3

Tonight I love you as the dashboard gleams
the perfect running of a million parts.
We are two people sharing the same dream,
an upholstered journey sleepier than seconal,
and to no end beyond its own fulfilling.
As soft upholstery loves the bodywork
it couches in; as the steel clip and
narrow black garter-band
loves
the refined and runnable threads they are pulling
with a tolerant intolerance of stresses, as
the mirror loves
the silence into which my future flashes.
The dream is where our love concludes and starts.
My love tomorrow I may stumble saying your name.

She watched it dully from her bed   the phone never stopped ringing
shambling polar bears   or Amundsen and Perry by a flag that streamed
a cyclonic absence of wind   the phone never stopped ringing
one huge step for man   thankyou   brief a presidential smile gleamed
thank you   thank you   yes a wonderful day for us all
they were halfway through EVA   extra-vehicular activity
once she whispered   agitatedly   no   that's impossible
mustn't come   please   no I don't know when it can be
impossible to be private   even   for a moment
they were   setting up   the seismometer
her eyes   were watching   the shadowy event
while her hand reached   for the vibrator
from the   crater sides they picked up lumps   of rock
it climbed her breasts   and stiffened   nipples
Houston reported it had received preliminary   shock
waves   her body recorded   a shrug of   ripples
there was no time for madness to touch down   each second of the count
was counted   the phone interrupted her   thank you   thank you
the vibrator infiltrated taut pyjama briefs   over   the venerean mount
exploring   finding nothing   into a cave   her eyes withdrew

4

I walked upon that lunar sea,
a second Adam to the flood;
the desert called Tranquillity
battered with meteorites. I stood,

as in Korea or Vietnam.
A barren plain that's drunk its gore.
In heaven too, I saw, the Ram
is slaughtered in a slower war.

Seconal was my only peace,
patented on our own dark star;
oxygen was love; to find out this,
strange, that I had to fly so far.

Unfiltered the sun's furnace roared;
a shadow was its fierce extreme;
a saviour round my body poured
cool water of Siloah's stream.

Even as the fish that rose to us
bore its own sea into our veins,
if we embrace the universe,
we must bring trees, we must bring rains.

We must bring dreams. I walked on ground
not sanctified by joy or sin.
Dream-emptiness stretched all around.
I wondered when life would begin.

Each second crammed with robot task;
EVA, the shadow I pursued;
tried to shut out, behind my mask,
the solitude's deeper solitude.

My rib in pain, as though some Eve
would spring, I slept but fitfully.
I felt it sad that I must leave
only my footprints on the sea.

5

To turn left, to turn right;
through me not myself alone
but a whole continent moves,
a world; the Old Glory planted on that moon
tonight; under the ice-cap polaris roves.
Every decision has to be right,
and without hesitation or remorse;
with this movement of a hand I set in motion
an irretrievable course;
even if it is wrong it will be right.
Even if I turn left, it will be right.
Fear adds salt; the velvet engine hums
adrenalin elation. Right.

6

A full moon rising over Finland
set the radar screens flickering holocaust.
Your crossed legs' nylon threads'
rising moonlit field of forces
unleashes a warhead.

7

I open the locket,
touch the lock of plain brown hair,
lock
so soft and so unopenable.
Fire fiercer than the consumption that
burns me burns me.

when from his eyes' portent-hungry   observatory dome
despairing calculations reckoned   that the universe
was running out was racing   for all its gathering momentum
of spirit its perpetually thickening noosphere round desire's
core to   meet head-on that anti-universe counter-time and –charge blight
to the wheat he should have strolled nonchalantly down from the   snow
line   picked fruit in the fields   then they might
have survived the impact   indeed her troubled face begged him to   do so
instead he panicked the blood's launching-pads   submitted her
to the pressure   of thrice-ten gravities   strapped in
through space-warp headed for   the metagalactic centre
mercilessly   the cunt-vortex   his desperation burning adrenalin
dervish dance of galaxies   catherine wheel of stars   the womb
hoping   like Diarmuid and Grania   Lancelot and Guinevere
whom they saw there   white   stunned   in their goldprowed tomb
and Tristan and his Iseult   in the black ship   that there
where it began its end might be delayed   by a few micro-
seconds   but no   he had dug his own grave   hearts
thumped at the last   the Word going out   she strapped below
him reaching hopelessly into her new dimension   new start

92

8

Your hair
black, black as the dead, wrong side of the moon,
comet tresses,
if my lips dare probe them, electrically alive as a storm of meteors,
and as mortal to my peace of mind.

Elipsed by darkness, the whites of your eyes gleam at me
like the coronae of a binary eclipse,
the cold, still chastity of your thighs where my teeth wander
is the Milky Way, galactic whirlpool and forge
which comes to us as cold, still, chaste light;

the constellations crazy,
their patterns haywire;
in the space of a week
you have flared from nothing into a supernova.

9

She touches her vagina;
And turns her gaze to the moon's blankness

10

Ophelia in your party-dress
the automobile's
skirts of steel,
heavy with their drink,
have pulled you to an unmelodious
and evil lay.

You are a flower crushed
on a dynastic battlefield;
you interrupted the swordthrust
meant for a greater.
Your death was doubtful;
you have become a brawl

over your maimed rites; an expendable sting
in an old curse, an argument
over your virgin crants;
but from your fair
polluted flesh
violets will spring.

11

Since you, my matchless donor, cut
me off as you cut off your hair,
--romantic folios you must shut,
hunting for more prosaic styles—
hacking it, dropping it in the fire,
the ripening bounty of three years
caught in the same tongue as my letters:
I take your letters and I cut
lying phrases from each page,
re-make them, strip on burning strip,
into each day a new collage,
a letter passionate and long,
re-seal it in an envelope
invisibly along the edge,
the flap still sealed from your moist tongue,
and send your letters to myself.

Since you, my soul and transplant, cut
me off like a long distance call
that ate into your youthful purse,
chequebook of marriageable beauty,
before I could pretend to reverse
the charge of love to my account,
mid-sentence in a blackmail plea,
as on the night I drove, through tears
contained by the mesmeric screen's
sickled, blindly springing rain,
your wraith still with me in the car
that you would never ride again;
coins became tranquillizers, call-
boxes dressing-stations, scarlet
along the highway, and to hear
your rising anger, easier than
the enormity of your withdrawal;
I made it grow, from each dead town;
all response gone, my ear still caught
some comfort in the throbbing phone,

I knew its green shape in your hall;
then, off the hook, at least it was
your air's indifference that spoke;
in a dark time I grasped at straws:

since all your lines went dead to me,
the hour each week your call came through
I arrange to get a call from time;
he rings reminding me it is
the hour I can expect your voice;
time who interrupted you
from me, and dragged all cables down,
makes small amends; you ring and ring;
time's tone was never pure as this;
for a wild minute love is true.

nine G.I.'s swinging down the rough road to Xuan Ngoc
where a full moon   is shining   floods the paddy fields
around it Surveyor turns   like the point of a clock-
hand   spin-off from that arrogance   falls
onto the nine G.I.'s nearing the hamlet of Xuan Ngoc
they rough up eight huts   and in the ninth   prepare
a girl for ritual rape   but under flashlight   they look
closely   long at her cunt and diagnose   VD they spare
her and go to the tenth hut   they find the young mother no harm
in her   and place   on father sister and two children   a guard
outside   her skinny resigned flesh has been nurtured on napalm
five have already screwed her   and the next two inside   are hard
when the father sets up a screeching howl and they grow afraid shoot
all five   next morning it is a chance of war   the major   forgives
spin-off from a skirmish with VC   the five-year girl   stirs   butt
of an M-14 smashes the story perfect   except   the mother lives
five G.I.'s swing down the dirt-track   to Cat Tuong
where a full moon   is shining   on the paddy fields
collect   in the hamlet a peasant-girl   to take along
to share   their   five-day mission   and their meals

12

Be great to fuck you on the dunes
where nothing grows but dry sandgrass,
your face a wayside stone of runes.

Lit by the headlights and the moon's
our instants throng on us and pass.
Be great to fuck you on the dunes.

Hand groping thigh, the future swoons
like a nude patient under gas;
your face a wayside stone of runes.

Midnight and engine-warmth maroons
us on Steel Island ringed by glass.
Be great to fuck you on the dunes.

Viola-husked the engine croons
monotones enigmatic as
your face. A wayside stone of runes

flicks by; the sharp rear-mirror prunes
from glare of might-be drifts of was.
Be great to fuck you on the dunes,
your face a wayside stone of runes.

13

i

This final privacy:
in love or war
to be shot
surrounded by cameramen.

Wait! Freeze.
A camera-plate is broken.
A fly settles on sweat.

ii

Colour-supplement
for a grey sunday;
Hollywood-jungle-technicolour.
Concentratedly,
staring down, this vietnamese
girl, man-handled, does up her
shirt-button;
her bewildered, lively, almost-
dead child on her arm.
It is
obscene of her.
No one should be shot
fastening a shirt-button
ten seconds before being shot,
(triangle of firm brown flesh).

whisper now   je t'aime   slide your hand   to meet his   so
lean over him   draw your hair back from where it veils your mouth
kiss him   where passion is edged with nuances of boredom   throw
your thigh across his in amends   lustfully   talk about   truth
in alphaville   your voice as close
to his ear as   this hidden receiver
is to yours   the lens   will   trace
intimately   the fall of the tear
that you will now evoke   I will   zoom right in
truth in alphaville   make up your own dialogue
whisper   while I whisper do you recall the inn
high in the mountain and higher still   the log-
cabin where we sheltered   my ring then on your finger
till you lost it in the snow and we scrabbled   on our knees   fill
your round tear with that slope and those cedars   I will linger
on it   while you talk   to your lover   of truth in alphaville
then we will cut   to an empty afternoon   cinema   rendezvous
with him distrait   unkempt and late   you will watch   this scene
then   cut   to   the premiere of this   where with your new
husband we shoot you watching you & your lover watching you on the screen

14

I watch you, glacial in mink,
enter on the arm of your husband,
imperious through the sighs
of your fans, the autographs.
Haughty, you take your seat;
your arm shrinks from his hand;
I whisper into your ear,
I am still crazy for you.
   Mink is as tender as steel
    in alphaville.

He is still crazy for you.
He watches you, late, uncombed,
with lateness on your mind
straight from your doctor's room,
enter the cinema's dark
afternoon, sit straight by him.
Neither yet flickers a sign.
You brush your hair from your eyes.
   Hair is as molten as steel
    in alphaville.

He watches you watching the screen
with never a glance at him.
He watches him loving you,
je t'aime   je t'aime   je t'aime
he whispers, now as then.
He is still crazy for you.
Your hands touch on the sheet,
like pack-ice, split again.
   Days are as cool as steel
    in alphaville.

Love is a cutting-room, all
images equally true,
I mix them all up in you,
au revoir becomes *je t'aime*
in the crystal at your ear,
as I direct your hand
to stretch for husband, lover;
the camera is crazy for you.
    A film can be cut like steel
        in alphaville.

Your hands in the pit of your back,
steel grapples to eyes of steel;
your breasts on hoardings star;
swiftly you brush your hair;
your husband is crazy for you.
Our son must be fetched from school.
Blinds of the late afternoon
are falling one by one.
    Light opens on the steel
        evening of alphaville.

You are the bathroom scales'
bland mutability;
the steel tape whips around
your breasts, your waist, your thighs,
inexorably as lovers;
the tape is crazy for you,
erecting your rasped nipples;
it hugs you into despair.
    You ghost into the steel
        slimlines of alphaville.

When, next autumn, next spring,
the houselights go down on this film,
who will be crazy for you,
whispering *je t'aime je t'aime*?
I whisper this in your ear:
stretch out your hand to him,
but remember our mountain-cabin;
preserve it in snow of your tear;
    converse on what is real
    in alphaville.

You are light falling on breasts,
you are a stocking's stretch,
you are the heel of a shoe,
you are a brush through hair,
you are a collar turned up,
you are the leaves you crunch,
you are the wheel of a car,
life is in love with you;
    you are the sad, steel thrill
    that steals through alphaville.

15

Ten o'clock and I have tossed
a last beer back out of the ice-box,
turned off the colour picture
and entered the bedroom with her,
a colour picture in her blue nightgown.
The spunk is the same,
when I   remember the woman in Xuan Ngoc,
if that was its name.

16

Da mi basia mille, deinde centum,
take, cut; take, cut; always something
dein mille altera, dein secunda centum,
ever-so-slightly imperfect sets us trying again;
dein usque altera mille, deinde centum,
sustained by the silence of many held breaths;
vivamus, mea Lesbia, atque amemus,
and if at times another voice whispers
soles occidere et redire possunt,
in your ear or mine, we are professionals,
nobis cum semel occidit brevis lux,
stretch out our hands again and again, to touch;
nox est perpetua una dormienda.
I think we shall perfect it in the grave.

17

Why does the steel, hygienic city
Hold so much dust?
Driving, to fetch my son from school,
tears streaming down my face,
will the curious indifferent standers-by
know it is a contact lens
and not despair?
Agonised, I flick it into my hand
Light as a waterdrop. Light.
Water-baby, it swims on the dead sea
of eyes.

Once, on the slopes of Mont Blanc,
I rubbed an eye unconsciously and
it flicked away, joined all the other snow-crystals
in the immense glacier,
till judgement.

Frozen, inseparable,
plastic and tear.
Longer than anyone
it will mourn for me.

we touched the world through the oily palms
of mute   petrol salesmen   in forest garages
we saw no headlines   sowing   unreal alarms
adjudged danger by our   own   steady gauges
what did we care in our favourite layby that the car
radio cut out in the midst   of Scarlatti   our lips
neverbreaking   our hearts still as near   and   as far
down the short wave band we followed   the eclipse
but on friday the scarlet lipstick you produced   as you prepared to leave me
turned black on your lips   saturday your skirt was no longer orange   a blue
moon shone through the windscreen on sunday on monday we crossed a city
where contrite hymnsinging shook the stadium   whether the lights said   go
we could not tell   till we reached the   no-speedlimit sign
tears did not cease to run your eyeshadow not green but ash
on tuesday   the sky was grey   with a black   sun
and today at noon   there is no colour except   a splash
of violet where your suspender belt arches round
a tuft of darker shadow   the shortest wave will
exceed these trees   soon   we wait   no sound
lit by black beams   a breeze strums   the aerial

18

Your face, beside me in the car and staring ahead,
has the beauty of the austere geometry
of gridroads, highways, underpasses, I
have cut from, imposed on, your innocent terrain.

Though tears star your cheeks like the few
rainsplashes left by the wiper on the windscreen,
the tears of foetuses, perhaps,
we cannot stop –the shoulder is hard.

Must lick up the cat's-eyes, endlessly,
as we do acts of love, slake our hungers where we pause.
The space between what I would like to give you, my
darling, and what I can, is this V, dividing the motorway

into two. One day you will slip away,
save yourself, as a car turns down a sliproad and
is gone. Then, I shall press my foot down
on the accelerator, harder, harder, and be gone.

19

I insist on watching you
piss. You laugh at my insistence.
If I knew why, I would know
the secret of the Mozart piano concerto
that has faintly followed us up the stairs.
How gaily, inexorably, it pursues its coda!

20

You sleep,
uncomfortably.   The car dreams
it holds bedrooms, dining-rooms, sun-rooms and creches.

21

When we lie together
meltingly
as the swan with Leda,
your eyes grow overfull
with children in Biafra,
children in Vietnam.
I am that brutal soldier,
My tenderness is rape.

22

All afternoon,
among stereos, plush carpets, among breasts and buttocks,
I have been making love to your eyes,
where it has been snowing frenziedly
and clearing to blue skies.
Your eyes have the stereogram's
mysterious fidelity,
that rises when I draw near,
fades when I move away.
My whisper caught in the one groove
of I love you,
like the old gramophone used to do.
All afternoon I have been making love to your eyes.
Now as we say goodbye,
and plan to meet tomorrow,
the snow has melted, retracted
into brambles and hedgerows and ditches.

so overcome   she did not hesitate   when the maintenance-
man   came to fix her heating   spoke through the door-
grill   but lifted the chain   she wrung her hands
crying   *the president has been shot*   stood in his white boiler-
suit   bag of heavy tools forgotten in hand   and stared
likewise at the screen   the motorcade broken
like a child's kicked line of cars   a shock shared
is more supportable   she was grateful not to be   alone
after the death arrives   he excused himself   work must be done
though new frontiers die   the debt collector must be paid
apartments must be made warm for single girls   in lonely Boston
JFK's city   through a halfopen door he watched   the motorcade
in playback   Jack smiling   and Jacqueline's proud face clear
of blemish nothing could stop   the next second's   horror
while with the other bloodstreaking eye   he watched disappear
his ordinary dull appearance   from the bathroom's silver mirror
picked up her drying nylons   when the wolfbane   blooms
under the high moon   even saints lock themselves   apart
and chain their doors   something loped through the room
as if it were snow   dry blood   tracks Jackie's skirt

23

'Even a man who says his prayers
before he sleeps each night,
may turn to a wolf when the wolfbane blooms
and the moon is high and bright.'

Chaos took one sharp bite at you,
invisibly he sped;
before your smile clamped to its mouth
the poison spread.

Soon as your blood rained on my skirt
like beast marks upon snow,
I knew you were in a forest where
to enter is to go

at once into its desolate heart;
none skirts its outer birches,
but penetrates past human call
to the black larches.

A change so absolute demands
more than those sinister
slight variations in your face,--
the cold –the stare – the leer.

Though I shall love you even till death,
if you returned tonight,
I'd bolt the door to your footfalls,
I'd shudder at your sight.

The Blue Shift

High over
Washington
she loses
her strained smile.
'Do not smoke,'
she tells us,
'while breathing
oxygen.'
Then whispers
for no-one
but the clouds,
'Nor suckle
your child while
aborting.'

She carries
her own bomb.
I watch her
skull broken
constantly
in hundreds
of thousands
of jigsaw
fragments. blank
and white as
Labrador.
But she re-
constitutes.

Her bones are
churned up by
many ploughs,
she becomes
cirrus-cloud,
madonna
of the rocks,
of cocktails,
but mostly
that pure blue,
her home is
never here.

More and more
        stars gather
        In the sky,
        too many
        prodigal
        suns, streaming
        home, over
        too many
        fields of time,
        to be fed
        by Lucy.

        She, the blue
        stewardess,
        has taken
        control and
        turned the craft
        back into
        the dawn, the
        darkness, to
        head for her
        own country.

Our journey
shadows time,
I can see
the watch-hands,
luminous,
of the blue
stewardess,
always at
six o'clock.

Her breath is
warm, comforts.
She shakes me
for the dawns
that never
come, keeping
me going
through black days.

The sound of
a river
beside us.
Once, in her
camera-
flash, the leap
of a fish.

Suddenly,
after days
of dark flight,
the white breasts
of mountains
look at us.
Where was a
house, faces,
at space's
edge, nothing
can haunt it.

She weeps for
nothing but
a child's shoe
by a well.

Light flies back
to the blue
stewardess.

She rides forth,
armed, erect,

dead, victrix.

Stands at the
bay in red.

Christ on Palomar

I have come out of
the cave, gulped the
thin air, entered
the white
dome

which is more silent, more
laden with awe than
the great temple
of the
prophets.

My brain reels under spectrographs
and maps of galactic
clusters. I was
a simple
carpenter.

Pulsars, quasars and neutron stars.
All such is beyond
me. I thought
only of
love,

creating them. I no longer
pretend to understand my
progeny, why this
particular, chance
design.

Plough, neversetting as the
cells of generation, why
did you sow
so prodigally,
demoniacally?

Andromeda's wheel, you are bland
as a pharisee, luminous,
doublemeaninged, as one
of my
        parables.

I know that, if the
faintest star fell or
were added, the
whole would
collapse

like a card-house, but I
no longer remember why.
I bear a
heavier cross
        now,

        the culpability, the burden of
        it all. I am
        blinded by the
        weight of
        stars.

        They stream towards me across
        fields of space-time, poor
        but confident: too
        many prodigal
        sons.